CliffsNotes®

St. Augustine's Confessions

By Stacy Magedanz, MLS

IN THIS BOOK

- Learn about the Life and Background of the Author
- Preview an Introduction to the Work
- Explore themes in the Critical Commentaries
- Acquire an understanding of the work with Critical Essays
- Reinforce what you learn with CliffsNotes Review
- Find additional information to further your study in CliffsNotes Resource Center and online at www.cliffsnotes.com

WILEY
Wiley Publishing, Inc.

About the Author

Stacy Magendanz is a librarian at Cal State San Bernardino. She has authored various literature and grammar study guides.

Publisher's Acknowledgments

Stacy Magedanz is a reference librarian in the Pfau Library at California State University–San Bernardino.

Editorial

Senior Acquisitions Editor: Greg Tubach
Project Editor: Marcia L. Johnson
Copy Editor: Tere Drenth
Editorial Assistant: Amanda Harbin

Composition

Indexer: TECHBOOKS Production Servicess
Proofreader: TECHBOOKS Production Services
Wiley Publishing, Inc. Composition Services

Published by:
Wiley Publishing, Inc.
111 River Street
Hoboken, NJ 07030-5774
www.wiley.com

Copyright © 2004 Wiley, Hoboken, NJ

ISBN: 0-7645-4480-2

Printed in the United States of America

10 9 8 7 6 5 4 3 2 1

1O/RX/QT/QU/IN

Published by Wiley Publishing, Inc., New York, NY

Published simultaneously in Canada

Library of Congress Cataloging-in-Publication Data
Magedanz, Stacy.
    CliffsNotes, St. Augustine's Confessions / by Stacy Magedanz.
        p. cm.
    ISBN 0-7645-4480-2 (pbk.)
    1. Augustine, Saint, Bishop of Hippo. Confessiones—Examinations—Study guides. 2. Christian saints—Algeria—Hippo (Extinct city)—Biography—Examinations—Study guides. I. Title: St. Augustine's Confessions. II. Title.
BR65.A62M34 2004
270.2'092—dc22
                                    2004002272
                                    CIP

Table of Contents

Life and Background of the Author 1

Introduction to the Work. 7

Critical Commentaries 15

Book 1, Chapters 1–5 16

Book 1, Chapters 6 and 7 18

Book 1, Chapters 8–11 20

Book 1, Chapters 12–20 23

Book 2, Chapters 1–3 25

Book 2, Chapters 4–10 27

Book 3, Chapters 1–5 29

Book 3, Chapters 6–12 31

Book 4, Chapters 1–3 34

Book 4, Chapters 4–13 37

Book 4, Chapters 13–16 39

Book 5, Chapters 1–7 41

Book 5, Chapters 8–14 43

Book 6, Chapters 1–10 46

Book 6, Chapters 7–16 49

Book 7, Chapters 1–21 52

Book 8, Chapters 1–4 55

Book 8, Chapters 5–12 57

Book 9, Chapters 1–7 60

Book 9, Chapters 8–13 63

Book 10, Chapters 1–25 65

Book 10, Chapters 26–34 68

Book 11, Chapters 1–31 71

Book 12, Chapters 1–31 74

Book 13, Chapters 1–38 77

Critical Essays. 80

CliffsNotes Review 85

CliffsNotes Resource Center 88

Index. 90

How to Use This Book

CliffsNotes St. Augustine's *Confessions* supplements the original work, giving you background information about the author, an introduction to the novel, a graphical character map, critical commentaries, expanded glossaries, and a comprehensive index. CliffsNotes Review tests your comprehension of the original text and reinforces learning with questions and answers, practice projects, and more. For further information on St. Augustine and *Confessions,* check out the CliffsNotes Resource Center at the end of this book.

CliffsNotes provides the following icons to highlight essential elements of particular interest:

Reveals the underlying themes in the work.

Helps you to more easily relate to or discover the depth of a character.

Uncovers elements such as setting, atmosphere, mystery, passion, violence, irony, symbolism, tragedy, foreshadowing, and satire.

Enables you to appreciate the nuances of words and phrases.

Don't Miss Our Web Site

Discover classic literature as well as modern-day treasures by visiting the CliffsNotes Web site at www.cliffsnotes.com. You can obtain a quick download of a CliffsNotes title, purchase a title in print form, browse our catalog, or view online samples.

You'll also find interactive tools that are fun and informative, links to interesting Web sites, tips, articles, and additional resources to help you, not only for literature, but for test prep, finance, careers, computers, and the Internet, too. See you at www.cliffsnotes.com!

LIFE AND BACKGROUND OF THE AUTHOR

The following abbreviated biography of St. Augustine is provided so that you might become more familiar with his life and the historical times that possibly influenced his writing. Read this Life and Background of the Author section and recall it when reading St. Augustine's *Confessions*.

Personal Background 2

Major Works 6

Personal Background

Saint Augustine of Hippo was born on November 13, 354, in the town of Thagaste, on the northern coast of Africa, in what is now Algeria. North Africa was part of the Roman Empire, though it was considered something of a backwater, far from the centers of imperial power. Augustine's father, Patricius (or Patrick), was a *decurio,* a minor official of the Roman empire. The position was far from glamorous, however, because a *decurio* was required to act as a patron for his community and to make up any shortfalls in taxes collected from the region. This responsibility probably kept a constant strain on the family's finances and may account for Augustine's assertions that his family was poor. Augustine had at least one brother, Navigius, and at least one sister, but little information is available about his siblings.

Patricius was a pagan, an adherent of the Roman civic religion. Augustine's mother, Monica (sometimes spelled Monnica), had been raised as a Christian. Although Patricius was only lukewarm about Christianity, he allowed Monica to raise the couple's children as Christians, and he finally converted to Christianity before his death. The example of his mother's fervent faith was a strong influence on young Augustine, one that would follow him throughout his life. In contrast, Patricius had relatively little influence on Augustine's character, and Patricius appears in the *Confessions* as a distant and vague figure.

Augustine showed early promise in school and, consequently, his parents scrimped and saved to buy their son a good Roman education, in the hope of ensuring him a prosperous career. He was sent to the nearby town of Madaura for further studies, but a lack of money forced him back home to Thagaste for a year, while his father tried to save more money for tuition. Augustine describes himself as a dissolute young man, unrestrained by his parents, who were more concerned with his success in school than his personal behavior.

When Augustine was about 16, his parents sent him to the university at Carthage, the largest city in the region. There he studied literature and poetry, in preparation for a career as a rhetor, a professional public speaker and teacher of rhetoric. Soon after Augustine came to Carthage, his father died, leaving Augustine as the nominal head of the family. In Carthage, he set up a household with a concubine, the mother of his son, Adeodatus, born about 372. During this period, he read the book that began his spiritual journey: Cicero's *Hortensius,* which he says inspired him with the desire to seek the truth, in whatever form he might find it. In Carthage, Augustine also encountered Manichaeism, the religion that dominated his life for the following decade. Augustine was attracted to Manichaeism's clear dividing line between good and evil, its highly intellectual mythology, and its strict moral standards.

After Augustine finished his studies, he briefly returned to Thagaste to teach, but soon went back to Carthage, where opportunities were more plentiful. Augustine became a successful public speaker and teacher. Encouraged by wealthy Manichee friends, he moved on to Rome in 383, hoping to advance his career. Rome proved to be disappointing, but Augustine's talents caught the eye of a Roman official who recommended Augustine for the position of public orator for the imperial city of Milan.

In 384, Augustine moved to Milan, where he heard the preaching of Bishop Ambrose. Augustine had always considered Christianity intellectually lacking, but Ambrose's application of Neo-Platonic ideas to the interpretation of Christian scripture, presented with Ambrose's famous eloquence, captured Augustine's interest. Augustine had been growing steadily dissatisfied with Manichaeism, and Ambrose's influence encouraged him to make a break with the Manichees. Augustine read the works of the Neo-Platonists himself, and this reading revolutionized his understanding of Christianity. Meanwhile, Augustine's career was flourishing, and his worldly prospects were bright. His mother had followed him to Milan, and she arranged an advantageous marriage to a Christian girl from a good family, requiring Augustine to send his concubine away. In the fall of 386, he had a conversion experience that convinced him to renounce his career and his marriage prospects in order to dedicate his life to God. He spent the winter with a group of like-minded friends, withdrawn from the world, reading and discussing Christianity. At Easter 387, he was finally baptized by Bishop Ambrose. On their way back to Africa, his group of friends and family was delayed at the coastal city of Ostia, where Monica fell ill and died. The account of Augustine's life as set out in the *Confessions* ends there, when Augustine was about 35 years old, but his life's work was only beginning.

In 389, Augustine returned to Thagaste, where he lived on his family estate in a small, quasi-monastic community. But Augustine's talents continued to attract attention. In 391, he visited the city of Hippo Regius, about 60 miles from Thagaste, in order to start a monastery, but he ended up being drafted into the priesthood by a Christian congregation there. In 395, he became the bishop of Hippo. He spent the next 35 years preaching, celebrating mass, resolving local disputes, and ministering to his congregation. He continued to write, and he became famous throughout the Christian world for his role in several controversies.

During this period, the Christian church in north Africa was divided into two opposing factions, the Donatists and the Catholics. In the early 300s, the African church had suffered Imperial persecutions, and some Christians had publicly renounced their beliefs to escape torture and execution, while others accepted martyrdom for their faith. After the persecutions ended, the Catholics re-admitted those Christians who made public repentance for having renounced their faith. But the Donatists insisted that anyone wanting to rejoin the church would have to rebaptized. Furthermore, they refused to recognize any priests or bishops except their own, believing that the Catholic bishops had been ordained by traitors. By the 390s, the conflict had erupted into violence, with Donatist outlaws attacking Catholic travelers in the countryside. At first, Augustine tried diplomacy with the Donatists, but they refused his overtures, and he came to support the use of force against them. The Roman government banned Donatism in 405, but conflict continued until 411, when hundreds of Donatist and Catholic bishops met for a hearing in Carthage before the imperial commissioner Marcellinus, Augustine's friend and a Catholic. Augustine, the former rhetor, eloquently argued the position of the Catholics, and Marcellinus decided in their favor. Donatism was suppressed by severe legal penalties. Augustine's vision of Catholicism as an institution that could thrive despite the imperfections of believers later became a definitive statement about the role and purpose of the church.

While the Donatist controversy was in full swing, a catastrophe struck the Roman world. In the year 410, Rome, the symbolic capitol of an empire that had dominated the known world for hundreds of years, was looted and burned by the armies of the Visigoths, northern European barbarian tribes. Many people throughout the empire believed that the fall of Rome marked the end of civilization as they knew it. In response, Augustine began writing his greatest masterpiece, *The City of God Against the Pagans,* which he worked on for 15 years. In *The City of God,* Augustine places the heavenly and eternal Jerusalem, the true home of all Christians, against the transitory worldly power represented by Rome, and in doing so, he articulates an entirely new Christian world view.

About the time of the fall of Rome, a movement called Pelagianism began in the church, calling for a fundamental renewal of spiritual and physical discipline. Its founder, a British monk named Pelagius, had read Augustine's plea to God in the *Confessions,* "Grant what you command and command what you will" (10.29). Pelagius was horrified by the apparent human helplessness that Augustine's statement seemed to imply. If human beings were incapable of being good without God's assistance, then what use was human free will? Pelagius argued that human beings could choose to achieve moral perfection through sheer force of will—and not only that they could, but that they must. Augustine, on the other hand, argued that no human being could expect to achieve anything like moral perfection; human will was irrevocably tainted by original sin. Christians could and should strive toward goodness, but they must also recognize their fallen state and their dependence upon the grace of God.

Once again, Augustine presented the argument that won: Pelagius was officially condemned in 416 and sent into exile. But Pelagianism remained influential, and Augustine spent his final years locked in a long-distance debate with an intelligent and articulate advocate of Pelagianism, Julian of Eclanum. Among other matters, Augustine and Julian clashed on the nature of human sexuality. Augustine identified the beginning of sexual desire with the beginning of human disobedience, Adam and Eve's original sin that tainted all humankind. Julian, however, could not accept the idea of original sin. He insisted that sexual desire was simply another of the bodily senses, and that the justice of God would not inflict punishment on the entire human race for the disobedience of one person.

In his debates with the Pelagians, Augustine broached another difficult issue, that of predestination. Because Augustine had argued that only the grace of God could move human beings toward salvation, the issue of how God chose those who would be saved became paramount. Augustine asserted that only a few people were saved, and only God knew who was saved and who was not. This assertion provoked a sort of revolt among several French monastic communities during 428. If one could undertake heroic acts of self-denial and spiritual commitment, as the monks had done, but still not know if one was saved, then what was the point of trying? In response to letters from the monks, Augustine acknowledged that predestination was a difficult issue, but he refused to yield the point. Predestination did not mean that human beings could safely give up spiritual striving; perseverance in faith was one of God's gifts to human beings.

In 429, north Africa was invaded by the Vandals, another barbarian tribe from Europe. The Vandals besieged the city of Hippo during the summer of 430; Augustine fell ill during August. According to his biographer, Possidius, Augustine spent the last days of his life studying the penitential psalms, which he had posted on the walls of his room, and weeping over his sins. He demanded that no one visit him, giving him uninterrupted time to pray. Augustine died on August 28, 430, at the age of 75, so he did not live to see the Vandals overrun Hippo in 431. The world Augustine had known, the old Roman Empire that had educated him even while he deplored it, was genuinely coming to an end. Augustine had an enormously influential role in shaping the world that replaced it, the Christianized civilization of Medieval Europe.

Major Works

Augustine was a prolific writer, producing more than 300 sermons, 500 letters, and numerous other works on a wide variety of topics. Many of these works have yet to be translated into English, although a massive translation project is currently underway. Conscious that he was leaving behind a large and influential body of work, Augustine set about organizing and revisiting his writings toward the end of his life, in his *Retractiones* (Retractions, 427). Although he never completed this task, his work and that of his friend and biographer, Possidius, left future readers with a well-documented list of Augustine's works.

Besides the *Confessions* (written 397–401), Augustine's other great classic work is *De civitate Dei* or *The City of God* (written 413–427), a monumental exploration of the end of pagan civilization and the role of Christianity in history. A brief selection of Augustine's other major works includes the following:

Enarrationes in Psalmos *(Explanations of the Psalms), 392–422*

De doctrina Christiana *(On Christian Doctrine), 396*

De trinitate *(On the Trinity), 399–422*

De Genesi ad litteram *(Literal Interpretation of Genesis), 401–415*

INTRODUCTION
TO THE WORK

The following Introduction section is provided solely as an educational tool and is not meant to replace the experience of your reading St. Augustine's *Confessions*. Read this section to enhance your understanding of the *Confessions* and to prepare yourself for the critical thinking that should take place whenever you read any literary work.

Introduction **8**

Augustine's Influences:
    Neo-Platonism **9**

Augustine's Influences:
    Manichaeism **11**

A Brief Synopsis **13**

Introduction

Augustine probably began work on the *Confessions* around the year 397, when he was 43 years old. Augustine's precise motivation for writing his life story at that point is not clear, but there are at least two possible causes.

First, his contemporaries were suspicious of him because of his Classical, pagan-influenced education; his brilliant public career as a rhetor; and his status as an ex-Manichee. In the midst of Augustine's prominent role in the Donatist controversies, he was suspected both by his Donatist enemies and by wary Catholic allies. One purpose of the *Confessions,* then, was to defend himself against this kind of criticism, by explaining how he had arrived at his Christian faith and demonstrating that his beliefs were truly Christian.

Another motivation may have been a bit of correspondence between Augustine's close friend Alypius and a notable Christian convert, Paulinus of Nola, a Roman aristocrat who had renounced the world and his immense family fortune upon converting to Christianity. Alypius wrote to Paulinus and sent him some of Augustine's works. Paulinus wrote back to ask Alypius for an account of Alypius' life and conversion. Alypius apparently conveyed the request to Augustine, which may account for the space devoted to Alypius' life story in Book 6.

The word "confession" has several senses, all of which operate throughout the work. Confession can mean admitting one's sins, which Augustine does with gusto, confessing not only his ambition and his lust but also his intellectual pride, his misplaced faith in Manichaeism, and his misunderstanding of Christianity. Confession also means a statement of belief, and this aspect is reflected in Augustine's detailed account of how he arrived at his Christian beliefs and his knowledge of God. Finally, confession means a statement of praise, and in the *Confessions,* Augustine constantly gives praise to the God who mercifully directed his path and brought him out of misery and error. In essence, the *Confessions* is one long prayer.

Structurally, the *Confessions* falls into three segments: Books 1 through 9 recount Augustine's life and his spiritual journey. Book 10 is a discussion of the nature of memory and an examination of the temptations Augustine was still facing. Books 11 through 13 are an extended exegesis of the first chapter of Genesis. The sharp differences between these three parts have raised many questions about the unity of the *Confessions.* Augustine himself commented in his *Retractiones* that the first ten books were about himself, and the other three were about scripture.

Some critics argue that, in fact, the *Confessions* has no unified structure, and Augustine simply proceeded without an overall plan for the work. Others think the final four books were tacked on at a later date. Still others have contended that the *Confessions* is, in fact, unfinished, and that Augustine intended the autobiographical portion simply as an introduction to a much longer work, either a full analysis of the book of Genesis (Augustine produced several of these analyses) or a catechism for new members of the church. Other critics have pointed to repeated themes across the three sections—the explorations of memory and time, in particular—in attempting to find unifying elements. Another way of looking at the structure of the *Confessions* is to view it as a journey in time: The first part recalls Augustine's past; the middle looks at his present situation; while the third part examines God's activity in history, from the beginning of the world, stretching up through the present and into the future. Nonetheless, many readers feel that the *Confessions* should have ended at Book 9, and even today, you can find copies that do not include the final four books.

The *Confessions* is always called a story of conversion. Augustine actually undergoes several conversions: to Manichaeism; to the pursuit of truth, with Cicero's *Hortensius;* to an intellectual acceptance of Christian doctrine; and finally to an emotional acceptance of Christian faith. Yet the term "conversion" is somewhat misleading. Even the young Augustine was never truly in doubt about the existence of God. Although he flirted briefly with the radical skepticism of the Academics, he was always certain, even as a Manichee, that Christ was the savior of the world. Augustine simply had the details wrong—in his view, disastrously wrong. Readers who do not share Augustine's religious beliefs will observe that he assumes God exists, so he finds the God he expects. Augustine's faith always colors his interpretation of events, and it is his measuring-stick for determining truth or falsehood. The *Confessions* is in one sense Augustine's personal story, but it is also a story with an almost mythological or archetypal appeal. Augustine is a kind of everyman, representing a lost and struggling humanity trying to rediscover the divine, the only source of true peace and satisfaction. As in a fairy tale, the outcome of the *Confessions* is never really in doubt; its hero is predestined, as Monica foresees, to find what he seeks.

Augustine's Influences: Neo-Platonism

Neo-Platonism has its roots in Platonism, the philosophy outlined by the Greek philosopher Plato (died 347 B.C.). One of the distinguishing features of Platonism is its assertion that the visible, tangible forms of the physical world are based on immaterial models, called Forms or Ideas. Tangible forms are transitory, unstable, and imperfect, whereas ideal Forms are eternal, perfect, and unchanging. Physical forms are many and diverse, but ideal Forms are single and unified. Platonism places a definite hierarchy of value on these qualities: Eternity is superior to the temporal; unity is superior to division; the immaterial is superior to the material. In Platonism, the fleeting physical world that humankind inhabits becomes a kind of flawed manifestation of a perfect and eternal model that can be perceived only by the intellect, not by the senses.

The Neo-Platonist philosophers Plotinus (c. 205–270 A.D.) and his disciple Porphyry (232–c.300 A.D.) expanded Plato's philosophical ideas into something more like a full-fledged cosmology. In the *Enneads,* Plotinus proposed a supreme divinity with three aspects. The "One" is a transcendent, ineffable, divine power, the source of everything that exists. It is complete and self-sufficient. Its perfect power overflows spontaneously into a second aspect, the Intelligence (Mind or *Nous*), which contemplates the power of the One. By contemplating the One, the Intelligence produces Ideas or Forms. The unity of the One thus overflows into division and multiplicity. These Forms are translated into the physical world through the creative activity of the World Soul. In the immaterial realm, the higher part of the Soul contemplates the Intelligence, while in the material realm, the lower part of the Soul acts to create and govern physical forms. According to Plotinus, the Soul, in descending from the immaterial to the material world, forgets some of its divine nature. All human individual souls, therefore, share in the divinity of the One and will eventually return to the divine realm from which they came, after they shed their physical bodies. Porphyry further developed Plotinus' ideas about the soul, asserting that individual human souls are actually separate from and lower than the World Soul. However, by the exercise of virtue and contemplation of the spiritual, the human soul can ascend from the lower, material realm, toward the highest good, the absolute beauty and perfection of the immaterial One. Augustine refers to this Platonic "ascent of the soul" in Book 9 of the *Confessions.*

Christians, for their part, were deeply suspicious of Platonism and of all the old pagan philosophies that Christianity had superseded. Nonetheless, Neo-Platonism had qualities that made it attractive to intellectual Christians. Neo-Platonism's three-fold model of divinity fit well with the Christian doctrine of the Holy Trinity. Neo-Platonism's stress on the transcendent, immaterial realm as the highest good also appealed to the ascetic streak in Christianity. Augustine found Neo-Platonism to contain all the major ideas of Christianity, with the important exception that it did not acknowledge Christ.

Augustine's Influences: Manichaeism

Augustine's other great spiritual influence was the religion of Manichaeism. Manichaeism was actually one of several Gnostic religions that flourished during this period. Gnostic religions (from *gnosis,* the Greek word for knowledge) promise believers a secret knowledge, hidden from non-believers, that will lead to salvation. Gnostic religions are also intensely dualistic, viewing the universe as a battleground between the opposing forces of good and evil. Like all Gnostic religions, Manichaeism held that darkness and the physical world were manifestations of evil, while light was a manifestation of good.

Manichaeism was founded by the prophet Mani (216–277 A.D.). Born in Persia, Mani was raised as a member of a Christian sect, but as a young man he received a series of revelations that led him to found a new religion.

Manichaeism was distinguished by its elaborate and detailed cosmology. According to Manichee myth, Light and Darkness originally existed separately, without knowledge of each other. The realm of Light, ruled by the Father, consisted of five orderly elements, called Fire, Water, Air, Ether, and Light. Its opposite, the realm of Darkness and matter, consisted of five disorderly elements. The Prince of Darkness then discovered the realm of Light and tried to conquer it. To defend Light, the Father produced the Mother of the Living, who in turn produced the Primal Man. Together with the five elements, the Primal Man went out to battle Darkness, but he was overcome, and demons of Darkness devoured his Light.

Light became trapped in evil physical matter. In order to rescue the Light, the Father created the Living Spirit. Together, the Primal Man and the Living Spirit battled the demons of Darkness. From the demons' corpses, they fashioned heaven and earth. They formed the sun and the moon from liberated bits of Light. Plants and animals were formed by the abortions and ejaculations of demons, as they tried to imprison the Light. The demons, overcome by lust, copulated, eventually giving birth to the first human couple, Adam and Eve. Salvation began when Adam received enlightenment about his true state from the Primal Man. One of the central beliefs of Manichaeism was the notion that every human being had two warring souls: one that was part of the Light, and another that was evil. Human sin was caused by the activity of this evil soul;

salvation would come when the good part of the soul was freed from matter and could return to the realm of pure Light. Through lust and the act of procreation, the Darkness tries to imprison more and more bits of Light within matter. Through Mani, the true revelation of knowledge will allow believers to liberate the Light within themselves and achieve salvation.

Manichee believers were of two types. The Elect, having reached spiritual perfection, practiced extreme asceticism, fasting regularly, following a strict vegan diet, and abstaining from all sexual activity. The Hearers, who made up the majority of believers, devoted themselves to caring for the Elect. Hearers were not held to the same rigorous standards of asceticism, but they were admonished not to have children, because doing so imprisoned more Light within matter. Manichees were not to eat any food derived from animals, because after it was dead and, therefore, empty of Light, animal flesh was nothing but evil matter. Eating fruits and vegetables, however, was a sacred act. Plants contained Light, and by eating them, the Manichee Elect freed the Light from bondage. Finally, no Manichee was to ever give food to an unbeliever, because by doing so, the Manichee would be imprisoning more bits of Light in matter. (Augustine mocks this belief in Book 3.10.)

Manichaeism had a strong missionary element, so it spread rapidly through the Middle East. Because Manichaeism had absorbed some elements of Christianity, it appealed to many mainline Christians. The Manichees, however, viewed Christianity as a flawed and incomplete religion. They were sharply critical of the moral failings of the patriarchs of the Old Testament, such as Abraham, David, and Moses. The Manichees pointed to Old Testament stories that described episodes of lust, anger, violence, and deceit to support their claims that the Old Testament God was really an evil demon, not a God of Light. The Manichees believed that parts of the New Testament were true, but they argued that the books of the New Testament had been altered to corrupt Christ's actual teachings, which reflected the true faith of Manichaeism. The Manichees specifically rejected the idea that Christ had been born from a human mother into a material body, because they viewed the body as evil. It was, therefore, also impossible that Christ could have suffered a physical death on the cross. Despite its popularity, Manichaeism was viewed as subversive by most civil authorities, and it was repeatedly banned. By the sixth century, Manichaeism had largely disappeared in the western part of the empire, although it survived well into the 14th century in parts of China, and religions similar to Manichaeism reappeared in Europe during the Middle Ages.

Augustine was a Manichee Hearer for almost ten years, and in the *Confessions,* he frequently refers to Manichaean doctrine and practices. Although they are distinctly different, Manichaeism and Neo-Platonism agree on a few basic ideas: that matter is evil (or at least inferior) and traps the human spirit; that human spirits contain some spark of the divine that must escape the material world to rejoin the ultimate Good; and that the true reality is not the one that people see around them. Unlike Neo-Platonism, Manichaeism was intensely materialistic. Where Neo-Platonism posits a completely spiritual, immaterial realm of being, even the Manichee Light seems to have a kind of substance, which was literally imprisoned within the bonds of physical matter.

A Brief Synopsis

The *Confessions* is a spiritual autobiography, covering the first 35 years of Augustine's life, with particular emphasis on Augustine's spiritual development and how he accepted Christianity. The *Confessions* is divided into 13 books. Books 1 through 9 contain Augustine's life story. Book 10 is an exploration of memory. Books 11 through 13 are detailed interpretations of the first chapter of Genesis, which describes the creation of the world.

Book 1: Augustine's infancy and early childhood. He falls ill and is almost baptized; he is sent to school to study Latin literature.

Book 2: Augustine's adolescence. He continues his studies; he becomes sexually mature; he steals pears with a group of friends.

Book 3: Augustine's early adulthood. He goes to Carthage to study; he reads Cicero's *Hortensius,* which inspires him with a love of wisdom; he encounters Manichaeism and becomes a Manichee.

Book 4: Augustine becomes a teacher of rhetoric; he takes a concubine; his grief at the death of a close friend drives him away from Thagaste.

Book 5: Augustine teaches at Carthage. He meets the Manichee bishop Faustus and is disappointed by Faustus' lack of knowledge; Augustine leaves Carthage for Rome and then Milan, where he hears the sermons of Bishop Ambrose, causing him to reject the teachings of the Manichees.

Book 6: Augustine learns more about Christianity but still cannot fully accept it; Monica arranges his marriage to a Christian girl, forcing him to send his concubine away.

Book 7: Augustine reads books of Platonist philosophy, which deepen his understanding of Christianity and the nature of evil; he finally accepts the truth of Christianity and repudiates Manichaeism.

Book 8: Augustine wavers in making a complete commitment to Christianity; after hearing various stories of conversion, he reaches a moment of spiritual crisis. Hearing a voice say, "Take and read," he picks up the Epistles of St. Paul and reads a passage that convinces him to give up his worldly career and devote himself to God.

Book 9: Augustine resigns his position and withdraws from the world. After his baptism, he sets out for Africa, but is delayed at Ostia, where Monica dies.

Book 10: Examination of memory and the temptations of the senses.

Book 11: Explanation of the first verse of Genesis, in which God begins the creation of the world; discussion of the nature of time and eternity.

Book 12: Explanation of the second verse of Genesis, with emphasis on the Word (Christ); discussion of how scripture may be interpreted.

Book 13: Explanation of the seven days of creation (the remainder of Genesis Chapter 1).

CRITICAL COMMENTARIES

The sections that follow provide great tools for supplementing your reading of the *Confessions*. First, in order to enhance your understanding of and enjoyment from reading, we provide quick summaries in case you have difficulty when you read the original literary work. Each summary is followed by commentary: literary devices, character analyses, themes, and so on. Keep in mind that the interpretations here are solely those of the author of this study guide and are used to jumpstart your thinking about the work. No single interpretation of a complex work like the *Confessions* is infallible or exhaustive, and you'll likely find that you interpret portions of the work differently from the author of this study guide. Read the original work and determine your own interpretations, referring to these Notes for supplemental meanings only.

Book 1 16

Book 2 25

Book 3 29

Book 4 34

Book 5 41

Book 6 46

Book 7 52

Book 8 55

Book 9 60

Book 10 65

Book 11 71

Book 12 74

Book 13 77

Book 1, Chapters 1–5

Summary

Augustine opens with a statement of praise to God; to praise God is the natural desire of all men. In calling upon God, Augustine shows faith, because he cannot call upon a God he does not know. God fills all of creation; God is perfect, eternal, unchangeable, all-powerful, and the source of all goodness. God is beyond Augustine's ability to describe; he asks God for the words to describe such greatness. Augustine pleads that he is too small and weak for God to come to him, but only God can aid him.

Commentary

Style & Language

Augustine opens his spiritual biography with a magnificent flourish of praise to God. The opening paragraph contains one of Augustine's most famous statements about humanity's relationship with God: "You stir us to take pleasure in praising you, because you have made us for yourself, and our heart is restless until it rests in you" (translation, Chadwyck). This pithy sentence summarizes a knotty proposition, one that is a major theme of Augustine's works and one that the rest of the opening simply restates and amplifies: Human beings naturally long to "rest" in God, to know God and to harmonize their wills with God's will. But because they are weak and sinful, humans can never hope to do this without God's assistance. In fact, all human impulses toward God have their origin in God.

Augustine has earned criticism throughout the centuries for this difficult proposition, which places so much emphasis on human weakness. Many readers have felt that Augustine denied human freedom of the will by portraying humankind as utterly passive, dependent upon God even for the impulse to love God. If human beings are powerless even to choose God without God's help, how can that choice have any moral value? Augustine, however, does not approach the problem in that way. Because Augustine's God is omnipotent, omniscient, and omnipresent, it is impossible for any part of the creation to exist outside of God. The nature of human sin, however, means that human beings can be blind to their dependency on God. This, in fact, is the story of Augustine's conversion: He was blind to God's truth, but God patiently drew him back toward that truth. This particular story is Augustine's alone, but as he presents it, it can also express the story of all humanity, painfully separated from God and always struggling to return.

The intimacy of the relationship between God and humanity is reflected in the intimacy of Augustine's narrative. In the *Confessions,* the conversation is always between "I," meaning Augustine himself, and "You," meaning God. In an important sense, Augustine's first and most important reader, or audience, is his God. In this opening, Augustine addresses God directly, as he does throughout the *Confessions,* so much so that he sometimes seems to forget the presence of his human audience.

Augustine's opening flourish of praise also reflects one of the three senses of "confession," that of confession of praise. The story of the *Confessions* is the story of Augustine's return to God, so it is appropriate that story should begin with Augustine's tribute of praise to the God he loves. In making a confession of praise, Augustine says, he is also demonstrating his faith, because he is not praising some distant or unknowable deity; God is as close to him as his own life and experiences, always working for Augustine's good, even when Augustine is unable or unwilling to recognize that truth. It is this confession of faith that keeps Augustine's focus on his human readers. By expressing his faith through the vehicle of his life story, Augustine hopes to bring his readers to a better understanding of God's grace.

Style & Language

Stylistically, these opening chapters pile question upon question, each one seemingly unanswerable and contradictory, but always resolvable by reference to God's compassion and generosity. In one long paragraph, Augustine attempts to describe the all-encompassing nature of God by expressing a series of opposites: God is hidden but always present; gathering to himself but not needing anything; recovering things lost but experiencing no loss. Augustine's elegant rhetorical style is on display throughout this opening section and throughout the *Confessions,* he will rely on almost musical passages as he attempts to express God's transcendent greatness and unfailing love. Augustine also makes constant use of language from the Christian Bible, weaving it into his text even when he is not directly quoting a particular passage; some translations make note of these references, but others do not.

Book 1, Chapters 6 and 7

Summary

Augustine discusses his infancy, which he knows only from the report of his parents. According to that report, Augustine became more aware and tried unsuccessfully to communicate his desires to the adults around him. Only God can say whether people exist in some form before infancy; Augustine says that his own knowledge is limited to what God reveals. God knows no past or future, only one eternal present. Even as an infant, Augustine was not free from sin. Observing infants, he notes that they throw tantrums if they do not get their way, although they are too weak to cause actual harm. Augustine thanks God for the good gifts of his body, his life, and his senses, gifts that reflect God's perfect ordering of all things.

Commentary

Chapter 6 introduces Augustine's infancy, although he has little to report about it, because he cannot remember it. He takes the occasion to make some observations about infants, which he concludes in Chapter 7. He emphasizes that everything that has sustained him, even the production of mother's milk, the instinct of a mother to feed her child, and a baby's desire for nourishment, are part of the natural order ordained by God and reflect God's goodness and generosity. He acknowledges the order God provides to the whole universe, of which God is the perfect and supremely beautiful model. This is an important point to remember when, as in Book 10, Augustine takes what appears to be a harshly negative view on the pleasures of the senses. In sharp contrast to the Manichees and the Platonists, Augustine ultimately affirms that the material world is good, because God made it, and the material world expresses God's perfect beauty and order.

Theme

However, Augustine does not share any sunny notions of the innocence of childhood. He believes in the idea of original sin, inherited by all human beings from the first man, Adam. Augustine is quick to clarify that God did not make sin; sin is humanity's responsibility. Augustine's views on original sin are complex, and he does not directly discuss the topic in the *Confessions*. Simply stated, original sin is the condition that inclines human beings to selfishness and disobedience, even when they may want to act otherwise. Original sin is evident in the tantrums and unreasonable anger of babies. In Augustine's view, even a baby may display murderous jealousy of his own brother at the breast. Characteristically, Augustine reasons from everyday existence that this behavior must be wrong, because similar behavior in an adult would be instantly condemned.

Theme

Augustine introduces the idea of language, the "signs" that he tried to use to communicate during his infancy his inward impulses to the external world. At this stage, Augustine's signs were woefully inadequate, but the inadequacy of language as a tool for genuine communication is one of Augustine's preoccupations, and it reappears in Chapter 8 and later in Books 10 and 11. As a man whose career was built on clever and skillful use of language, often for amoral purposes, Augustine displays ambivalence about language itself. Language is necessary to human life in society and to transmitting the knowledge of God, but it is also easily perverted and corrupted.

In this discussion of infancy, Augustine deliberately ducks the question of whether human beings exist before birth or even before conception, claiming that such things are simply beyond the knowledge that God has seen fit to reveal. Specifically, Augustine is avoiding making a statement about whether the soul exists prior to its union with the human body. Both the Neo-Platonists and the Manichees believed that the soul existed in a divine, immaterial realm before entering its prison of human flesh in the material world. Endorsing this view would have left Augustine open to accusations that he was still a Manichee, or that he was a Neo-Platonist with the trappings of Christianity. However, Augustine does not specifically refute this viewpoint; he simply refuses to address it, because it is something beyond what God has revealed to human knowledge.

On the subject of mysteries beyond human understanding, Augustine takes the opportunity to discuss God's eternity; that is, human beings perceive time as moving in a linear fashion, past, present, and future, but to God, all times are one simultaneous present, one "today." This discussion of human time versus God's time reappears as Augustine examines the creation of the world in Book 11.

Book 1, Chapters 8–11

Summary

Augustine discusses his childhood. During that time, by observing how adults use words and using the power of memory, Augustine grasped that a word indicated a certain thing. In learning language, Augustine joined human society. Next, he was sent to school. When he was lazy, he was beaten. He found punishment miserable, although adults only laughed at his misery. Augustine loved to watch adult sports and shows, and he was punished for this, as well.

As a boy, Augustine was introduced to Christianity. When he fell seriously ill, he pleaded to be baptized. His mother would have arranged it, but Augustine got better, so his baptism was postponed. Augustine laments that he was not baptized as a child, but his mother thought it better to let him face the temptations of adolescence before baptism.

Commentary

Augustine's childhood is the subject of this section. His description of how he learned to speak is charmingly simple, but it displays Augustine's fine eye for observation of human behavior. It is notable that he describes his motivation for learning to speak as a selfish one: He wanted to get others to obey his wishes.

Language is Augustine's key to entry into human society, and it becomes his key to worldly success. He makes clear from the beginning that his parents had only the most shallow goals for promoting his education; namely, getting him into a good career as a rhetor. The follies of children, contrasted satirically with the follies of adults, form another theme of this section, pointing up the shallowness of Augustine's education and the futility of desire for wealth or fame: The masters who punish him share the same childish sins of jealousy and anger that he does, and the parents who disapprove of his love of theatrical shows punish his idleness only so that he can grow up to be as rich as the men who stage the shows. However, Augustine admits that education itself is good, and he might have put his training to better use. Augustine devotes considerable space to the beatings inflicted on him by his schoolmasters. He is drawing on stock literary devices in lamenting the miserable life of a schoolboy and in comparing the "minor" affairs of children to the supposedly "major" affairs of adults, but the forcefulness of his description suggests that he genuinely disapproves of corporal punishment.

Nonetheless, Augustine specifically states that he deserved his punishment, not because he was lazy or stupid, but because he disobeyed his parents and teachers. Augustine's insistence on this point is easier to understand if you recall that disobedience is at the foundation of all human sinfulness. By emphasizing his disobedience, Augustine draws comparisons between his own childish impulses and the condition of all human beings.

As Augustine helpfully explains, it was a common practice in the early Christian church to defer baptism, a major Christian sacrament, for as long as possible, even to the end of one's life. Baptism was regarded as cleansing the believer from all previously committed sins and, therefore, any sins committed after baptism would be much harder to forgive. This explains Monica's pious reluctance to baptize her son after his illness improves, because he has a long life of sins looming in front of him. Augustine strongly disapproves of the practice of deferring baptism, feeling it would have been better to bring him to God's salvation than to let him go on sinning because he was young. Baptism would not have kept him from sinning, but for Augustine, forgiveness of sin is not a single, all-or-nothing event. Because all human beings are subject to the influence of original sin, they constantly sin and are constantly in need of God's forgiveness and grace. Once again, Augustine draws an analogy from everyday life: No one would ever recommend letting a sick man get worse, merely because he was not completely cured yet.

This chapter marks the first real appearance of Augustine's family, beyond the fuzzy images of his mother and nurses feeding and caring for him in infancy. His mother Monica steps forward as a woman of strong character and already an enormous influence on young Augustine, particularly in her example of Christian faith. He praises Monica's piety, particularly because she had to contend with a husband who was still a pagan, but the portrait of her is not uniformly glowing. She lets an important opportunity to save Augustine pass by, and this is the only time she does so in his life. Augustine understands her reasoning, but expresses his disappointment. In comparison, Augustine's description of his father is that of someone distant, as if his father's influence is scarcely felt in the dominating presence of his mother. At least his father does not forbid his mother to practice her religion, allowing all the children to be raised as Christians. Still, it is Monica who gets Augustine's praise for being obedient to her husband, because in obeying him she was obeying God's will.

Glossary

(Here and in the following chapters, difficult words and phrases, as well as allusions and historical references, are explained.)

catechumen   a Christian receiving instruction in the faith but not yet baptized. As the child of a Christian mother, Augustine was at least nominally a catechumen from early childhood onward.

sign of the cross   a gesture of blessing; a priest would bless catechumens by making the sign of the cross over them.

salt   salt was placed on the tongues of new catechumens. Salt was frequently used as a protection against evil spirits, and it also recalled Christ's admonition to the church that "you are the salt of the earth" (Matthew 5:13).

Book 1, Chapters 12–20

Summary

As a child, Augustine hated being forced to study, and those who forced him had only empty wealth and glory in mind. Augustine reports that he loved reading Latin literature but always hated Greek. He disliked learning the mechanics of Latin, but it was better than reading vain stories, which directed Augustine's emotions to wrong ends. According to Augustine, traditional education teaches immoral fictions, encouraging readers to sin. Augustine says it was not surprising that he wandered away from God when he was expected to follow these empty examples. Like the Prodigal Son, he was blinded by wickedness and could not find his way back to God. Augustine excelled in school and enjoyed earning approval from his elders. Nonetheless, he was a troublemaker at school and at home. God gave Augustine many admirable talents and qualities, but he sinned in looking for truth and beauty in the world, rather than in God, and this led Augustine into confusion.

Commentary

Book 1 closes with Augustine's lament over his empty education. He is sharply critical of the literature-based curriculum of his childhood, which valued artistic style over moral content. Already, Augustine is being trained to manipulate words to produce emotional responses in an audience, but these responses are without any real substance, or worse, are directed toward ends that are actually immoral. Augustine seems to have had a particular weakness for theater (see Book 3), based mainly on the strong emotional responses it aroused. He learned as an adult to condemn these empty emotional displays. How can it be right, Augustine argues, for you to weep over a fictional tragedy, but feel no sorrow for your own sins, or to condemn someone for a minor academic error, but fail to condemn your hatred of your fellow human beings? Education without moral content leads only to further estrangement from God, entangling humans in a world whose values are fundamentally skewed.

Augustine describes himself as a very bad little boy: He lies; he steals; he tattles on his friends; he cheats in order to win; and he is angry if anyone else employs those same tactics on him. It takes only a little imagination, however, to see him behaving no worse than any other bright and energetic child at school. All of his faults are minor if you see them in this light, but for Augustine, these faults are evidence of his fundamental sinfulness, and he cannot dismiss them as innocent childhood incidents. Augustine does take time to describe some of his good personal qualities: He loves the truth; enjoys his friends; is intelligent; and has a good memory. It is also clear that he loves to be praised and to earn the approval of the adults around him; this quality in adulthood will become part of the ambition that drives him toward a successful career as a rhetor. Ultimately, however, Augustine's good impulses are misdirected. Instead of looking for the true source of beauty, happiness, and truth, which is God alone, he looks for these things in the world around him, where the warped values of his education dominate.

Glossary

Aeneas and Dido   Aeneas was the legendary founder of Rome and the hero of Virgil's *Aeneid*. Dido, the queen of Carthage, kills herself after being abandoned by Aeneas.

Troy, ghost of Creusa   Creusa, Aeneas' wife, died trying to escape from the besieged city of Troy. In Book 2 of the *Aeneid*, Aeneas describes how he met her ghost as he also fled.

Homer   Greek poet and author of the *Odyssey*.

Terence   Latin playwright, author of six comedies written in the 160s B.C. Augustine is quoting from Terence's play *The Eunuch*.

Jupiter and Danae   Jupiter is the king of the gods in Roman mythology. To seduce Danae, a human woman who had been locked up in tower by her father, Jupiter turned himself into a golden shower and rained into Danae's lap.

Juno   the queen of the gods in Roman mythology. Augustine's contest involved an angry speech Juno gives in Book 1 of the *Aeneid* after Aeneas escapes from her.

Prodigal Son   the subject of one of Christ's parables (Luke 15:11–32). The son of a rich father, he demands his inheritance, and then squanders it in dissolute living. Destitute and humiliated, he finally returns home to beg from his father, who joyfully takes him back.

Book 2, Chapters 1–3

Summary

Augustine turns to his adolescence and describes his sins of lust. At sixteen, he came home from school for a year while his father tried to raise money to send him to a better school in Carthage. Augustine was by then sexually mature, which made his father happy, but worried his mother, who cautioned him against committing fornication and adultery. Augustine scoffed at her advice and enjoyed boasting to his friends about his sexual exploits, even if he had to exaggerate for effect. His mother could have arranged a marriage for him to give him a legitimate outlet for his sexual urges, but she feared that marriage at that time would hurt his chances for a successful career.

Commentary

Theme

Augustine's account of his sexual sins is one of the most famous features of the *Confessions,* and that account begins here in Book 2, as Augustine becomes a teenager. Augustine's attitude toward his sexual urges is always deeply problematic, and a reluctance to give up sex is one of the last, painful obstacles to his full conversion. Here, however, Augustine gives a typically nuanced analysis of his sexual sins. His initial impulse, to love and be loved in return, is a good one, but once again, his good impulses are misdirected toward bad ends. He is unable to distinguish between physical love, which satisfies only lust, and the spiritual love of friendship and companionship, which satisfies the heart and the mind. With psychological acuteness, he also observes that part of his impulse toward promiscuity involved bragging rights with his group of friends, who took just as much pleasure in telling stories about their exploits as in the acts themselves. Given Augustine's statement that he sometimes had to exaggerate so that he would not seem too innocent to his buddies, one has to wonder exactly how bad his behavior really was.

The attitude of the early church toward sexuality of any kind was extremely negative, and Augustine reflects this attitude as he quotes advice against sex and marriage from the letters of the Apostle Paul.

Complete celibacy was held up as the highest goal for a Christian, and marriage was a less admirable alternative, suitable only for those who could not fully control their sexual impulses and, therefore, required a "legitimate" outlet for them. Even within marriage, sexual activity was to be reserved solely for the conception of children, and not enjoyed for its own sake. Augustine describes his time of promiscuity as a period of misery, in which his suffering was reflective of God's gentle correction, although at the time, Augustine was still too ignorant to understand it.

Character Insight

The reaction of Augustine's parents to his developing sexuality is telling: Patricius, although nominally a Christian catechumen at this point, is thrilled at the prospect of having a grandchild, and Patricius' delight at seeing evidence of his son's sexual maturity—while Augustine is naked in a public bath—seems more than a little crude. Monica offers pious motherly advice about chastity, but no more than this, even though she is aware of Augustine's behavior. Augustine is careful to point out that God was speaking to him through his mother, though as a typical teenager he shrugs off her warnings. However, Augustine laments that his parents both refused to rescue him from his sin by arranging a legitimate marriage for him. The reason was simple: Marriage to a country girl would have held him back from a brilliant career, where he could make a more socially advantageous marriage to an heiress. (In fact, Monica arranges just such a marriage for him in Book 6.)

The dynamics of Augustine's family life are on display in this section, as he speculates about his parents' wishes for him. Worldly ambition for Augustine (possibly their oldest son) seems to drive both parents' actions, but Augustine reserves his sternest disapproval for Patricius, apparently because Patricius shows no awareness that there is any "success" beyond the shallow rewards that the world can give. Augustine notes with irony that everyone praised his father for making so many financial sacrifices for Augustine's education, even though his father cared nothing about the vicious character such an education would develop. Augustine presents Monica as more scrupulous. She feels that a literary education will at least do no harm to Augustine's spiritual life, but she, too, is anxious to see her son succeed. Augustine praises his mother's piety and faith, but there is still a note of criticism as he reports on her failure to save him from his sexual sins by seeing him properly married.

Book 2, Chapters 4–10

Summary

With a gang of his friends, Augustine sneaks into an orchard at night and steals a load of pears. He did not want the pears, nor was he motivated by any self-interest. He simply enjoyed the act of doing wrong for its own sake. Trapped in misdirected love of earthly goods, the soul separates itself from God and tries to demonstrate its power over God by breaking God's laws. Augustine knows also that he would never have committed the theft alone. He withdraws from contemplation of his crime in disgust, taking refuge in God's peace.

Commentary

Theme

Readers may wonder why Augustine lavishes such anguished and intense self-scrutiny on what sounds like an otherwise minor bit of juvenile delinquency: the theft of some pears from a neighbor's orchard. However, do not accept the description at face value, because Augustine is using this episode to stand both as a generic example of all the other sins committed in his youth and of the common sins of humanity. Viewed this way, Book 2 points up two types of sin: The first, lust, is an example of misdirected love, a confused attempt to seek satisfaction in transitory things that can never truly satisfy.

The second type of sin, the love of wrongdoing simply for the doing of it, is more difficult to classify. Scrutinizing his actions, Augustine expresses dismay at his complete lack of logical motivation for the theft. Every crime has a motive, he says, and it is easy to understand crimes motivated by greed or some other self-interest. But Augustine did not even want the pears. Augustine's theft had no excuse beyond the illicit thrill of doing wrong.

Augustine concludes that this sin is a kind of rebellion against God's omnipotence, a perverse attempt to demonstrate the soul's imagined self-sufficiency. Even by attempting to deny God's omnipotence, the sinner imitates it, thereby proving that nothing is outside of God's fullness and dominion. Like the misdirected love of others that is at the root of lust, misdirected love of self is at the root of rebellion.

The theft of the pears has further implications if you view it as generic rather than specific. Humankind's fundamental disobedience and fall from grace involved the improper taking of fruit from a tree in a garden, as recounted in the story of the Fall (Genesis 2–3). Later, Augustine's final conversion takes place under a fruit tree in a garden, standing in contrast to a present episode of sin as well as to Adam and Eve's. Some scholars have seen the pear theft story as simply an extended metaphor for the sin of promiscuity, the theme begun in the first part of Book 2. This interpretation also has links to the story of Adam and Eve, because humanity's Fall was believed to have included a fall from sexual innocence. Augustine himself describes sin in Book 2.6 as the soul's "fornication" against God.

As much as he is concerned with analysis of his own individual sins, Augustine is always concerned with the life of human beings within society and here, he runs into a wall. He knows that he would never have committed the theft if he had not been with a group of his friends. In contemporary terms, he is aware of the influence of peer pressure, subtle and unspoken, on his own behavior. Augustine tries to explain exactly how this social pressure operates. What is it about human beings in groups that makes them so susceptible to irrational impulses, impulses they would never act upon if they were alone? For Augustine, who so deeply values friendship, this remains an unsolvable problem. People in groups can both support each other in good—as his little community of friends later does at Cassiciacum—and egg each other on in evil, as his gang of boyhood friends does at the orchard.

Glossary

Catiline d. 62 B.C.; Roman conspirator. Augustine quotes from the history of Catiline's career by Sallust (c. 86–35 B.C.), in which Catiline is represented as an archetypal villain.

Book 3, Chapters 1–5

Summary

In school at Carthage, Augustine continues to be lost in carnal desires. He enjoys the vicarious suffering he could experience by watching theatrical shows; he stops to consider the agonies of love. He has begun his studies of law, and he keeps company with a group of unruly students, although he disapproves of their malicious acts.

In the course of his studies, Augustine reads Cicero's *Hortensius,* and it changes his entire outlook. Reading the book excites his love of philosophy, and he resolves to pursue true wisdom. Augustine decides to study the Bible, but finds it lacking in literary style.

Commentary

Now about 18 years old, Augustine is studying to become a lawyer and living a life not so different from that of a modern college student. He is away from home, on his own in a large city, doing well at school, leading an active social life, and going to plays. He reports that he fell in love, although he does not say with whom; many readers have assumed this to be his unnamed concubine. In contrast to Book 2, Augustine is beginning to resist peer pressure. He is acquainted with a group of upperclassmen who take pleasure in tormenting shy, younger students. Augustine does not completely disassociate himself from this group, but he disapproves of their actions and refuses to participate in their cruelty.

Theme

In Carthage, Augustine continues to be plagued by his sexual impulses and by his misdirected desire for love. The torments of sexual desire are a prominent theme of the *Confessions,* and Augustine often seems to identify all human sin with lust, or in his terms, "concupiscence." "Concupiscence" is ultimately a selfish and excessive desire for anything, not only for the pleasures of the flesh, and Augustine constantly identifies misdirected desire as the root cause of his wanderings from God. Augustine has frequently been accused of equating sex with original sin; the sexual act itself for him becomes a kind of infection that contaminates with original sin the children it conceives. In the *Confessions,* this connection is not directly stated, but it is reflected in Augustine's attitude toward sex as a sinful impulse that reason cannot control, an intractable habit that only the grace of God allows him to break.

Augustine has already shown his weakness for the emotional appeal of fiction in Book 2, and now it manifests in his reaction toward theater. As with fiction, Augustine disapproves of the empty emotional reactions that theater creates in the audience. In essence, Augustine views fiction and theater as emotional titillation; merely producing sensations, but having no moral ends. This discussion of the empty suffering provoked by theater leads Augustine into a dense argument that compares the suffering produced by genuine love (compassion) to the suffering produced by carnal love (passion) and the false suffering produced by theatrical shows. Augustine clarifies that suffering for the sake of others is not wrong, because pity (compassion) is always linked with suffering. But the enjoyable suffering of love is easily perverted, and even human compassion can proceed from mixed motives. Only God's compassion is completely pure.

Character Insight

Augustine's encounter with the *Hortensius* is one of the critical turning points in his life, and it is often referred to as his "first conversion." Cicero was one of the most-studied classical Latin authors, and his rhetorical style was considered near perfect, a model for all students to imitate. The *Hortensius* itself has not survived, and much of what scholars know about it comes from quotations in Augustine's works. It was a defense of the study of philosophy, exhorting readers to look for truth in whatever guise truth may take. As a bright, impressionable young man, apparently already feeling a sense of spiritual emptiness, Augustine takes this advice directly to heart and resolves to pursue true wisdom from now on. But Cicero is a pagan, and having been raised Christian, Augustine feels he should look to his religion for answers. His education has led him to value elegance of expression, and the Bible is too simple and homespun for his refined tastes. Looking back, Augustine concludes that he was too intellectually conceited to see the complex meanings behind the simple words. Augustine's dislike of the plain-spoken Christian Bible has major consequences for his burgeoning spiritual life, as he soon becomes attracted by a more refined and intellectual species of Christianity: Manichaeism.

Character Insight

In this section you also learn, in an almost off-hand remark, that Patricius has been dead two years, and Monica is now supporting Augustine at school. His father's death appears to have made very little impression on Augustine, and at any rate, it is not important to the tale of Augustine's conversion.

Book 3, Chapters 6–12

Summary

Still searching for the truth, Augustine encounters the Manichees. He is taken in by their objections to the literal sense of the Bible and by the physicality of their mythology, because he fails to understand that only the spiritual reality is the true one, while the physical reality is merely the reflection of spiritual reality. He also does not realize that right and wrong are not determined by the customs of different places or times but by the unchangeable law of God. Augustine considers the nature of sin: Some sins offend God's laws, and some sins offend others by causing harm or suffering. Sin springs from three causes: lust for power, carnal lust, and lust of the eyes. But because Augustine is ignorant of all of this, he accepts the absurd mythologies of the Manichees as the literal truth.

Meanwhile, Monica is grieved by Augustine's conversion to Manichaeism. She has a dream in which she sees herself and Augustine standing on the same measuring stick. She goes to a bishop to plead with him to talk to Augustine, but he tells her that Augustine will recognize the errors of the Manichees soon enough on his own.

Commentary

Having found Christian scriptures too simple to be satisfying, Augustine turns to the more complex mythology of Manichaeism. Augustine explains his attraction to Manichean doctrine in terms of misplaced literalism—based on a literal reading of the Bible, the Manicheans accused Catholic Christianity of absurdity and immorality.

Character Insight

Here, as he so often does throughout the *Confessions,* the mature Augustine looks back to analyze and explain the errors of his youthful beliefs. Augustine's answer to the Manicheans' literal interpretation comes to him in the form of Platonism. Augustine's insistence on spiritual truths rather than literal interpretation allows him to answer the Manichees' accusations that the heroes of the Old Testament behaved immorally. Augustine responds with an interesting bit of moral relativism: God's laws never change, but throughout history, different human societies have applied those laws as was appropriate to their circumstances. Augustine allows for variations in local customs and practices, so long as the essence of God's law is not violated. Societies may determine what is acceptable behavior, but God's law is always supreme. When God commands something contrary to human custom, human custom must change.

This exploration of morality leads Augustine into a discussion of the types and origins of sin. Sinful acts either offend God's law, injuring the self, or they seek to injure others—whether physically or spiritually. Sin proceeds from three sources: pride, lust, and curiosity (or *curiositas,* Augustine's Latin term). *Curiositas* can literally mean intellectual curiosity, a restless seeking for things that are not God, but it is also closely related to Augustine's love of theater and other empty spectacles, and to the seduction of the visual that he discusses in greater detail in Book 10. All three of the causes of sin are varieties of concupiscence, excessive and mistaken desires for the transitory good offered by the material world.

Augustine refers to a few bits of the complex Manichean mythology, which he compares to the empty fictions of literature he was still studying at that time. By doing so, he identifies the appeal of Manichean mythology with the sin of *curiositas:* intellectual pride and a delight in meaningless spectacle that diverts one from the truth.

Monica reappears in Augustine's narrative as a model of Christian motherhood and almost as a personification of the Church herself. She reprimands her wandering son, although he ignores her. All the while, she remains simply and steadfastly faithful, constantly praying for her son's return to the faith. Like the Church, she becomes the vehicle for the communication of God's will, receiving two messages about Augustine that she believes come directly from God.

The first of these is a dream in which a young man reassures her that Augustine will eventually join her on the "rule," the straight way of correct Christian doctrine. Dreams were a recurring interest of Augustine's. Although he is often concerned with their capacity to deceive by imitating reality (as in 4.6, where he talks about food in dreams, and 10.30, where he considers sexual dreams), he also shared the general belief of his time that dreams could be direct communications from the divine.

Literary Device

Monica's second communication from God comes in the form of a message from an ex-Manichee bishop. The bishop is a foreshadowing of the mature Augustine, who is himself a bishop and ex-Manichee. Monica tearfully begs the bishop to talk to her son, and he responds with a famous admonition: "It cannot be that the son of these tears should perish" (translation, Chadwyck). These two messages close Book 3 on a note of hope. Although he will remain a Manichee for nine years, Augustine's return to the Church is inevitable, and the search for wisdom he has begun so tentatively will be successful. The Augustine who speaks for most of Book 3 is the Augustine who can now look back clear-eyed at the mistakes of his youth. God has already heard Monica's prayers for her son's rescue, but it will take time for God's will to be worked out in Augustine's life.

Glossary

husks   After he wastes his inheritance, the Prodigal Son is reduced to eating the "husks" or scraps that are fed to pigs. Augustine uses this as a metaphor for the literature he was teaching to his students—he could not find spiritual nourishment in the "husks" of pagan fiction.

Medea   a sorceress of Greek mythology; she flies through the air in a chariot pulled by dragons.

Five Elements, Five Caves of Darkness   a reference to Manichean mythology.

Solomon's allegory   King Solomon was believed to be the author of the Old Testament book of Proverbs. See Proverbs 9:17, where the "woman" is Folly or Ignorance.

Abraham, Isaac, Jacob, Moses, and David   patriarchs of the Old Testament.

foot   a metrical unit in poetry.

Sodom   Biblical city destroyed by God (Genesis 18:20–19:25). The Sodomites were traditionally believed to have practiced homosexuality.

ten-stringed harp   the Ten Commandments (Exodus 20).

Book 4, Chapters 1–3

Summary

From ages 19 to 28, Augustine is a teacher of rhetoric and an adherent of Manichaeism, both false occupations. During this time, he lives with a woman and has a child by her. He is faithful to her, although their relationship was based on sex, not on friendship. He despises soothsayers, but he continues to consult astrologers and to practice astrology himself, despite the advice of a wise friend that astrology is phony.

Commentary

By now, Augustine is an adult, teaching rhetoric back in his hometown of Thagaste. He continues as a Manichee Hearer (also called Auditor), meaning he is a disciple, although not one of the most highly placed in the sect, one of the Elect. He identifies both the public and the private aspects of his life as based on deception. Just as he is deceived by the false words of the Manichees, he teaches his students to deceive others with words in the courts of law. He still has a conscience, however, as he prefers to teach "virtuous" students when he can find them, and he tries to impress his students with the idea that it is better to let a guilty criminal go free than to condemn an innocent man to death. Augustine's attacks of conscience partly explain his abhorrence of soothsayers, who offer to sacrifice animals to various spirits in order to assure Augustine's success in public rhetorical contests. John J. O'Meara observes that as a Manichee, Augustine would have objected to killing any living creature. Augustine may also have considered that the demons the soothsayer invoked were evil.

Augustine is not as adverse to astrology, which does not make appeals to evil spirits, but relies on an apparently rational observation of natural phenomena, namely the movements of the stars, in order to predict future events. Manichaeism also had its own kind of astrology, because its myths emphasized the roles of the sun and moon. Although he does not discount God's ability to intervene in the natural order in miraculous ways,

Augustine deeply values rationality. He believes that natural order reflects God's divine order and that reasoned contemplation of the lower order of the physical world can lead the mind to the higher order of spiritual truth. Astrology's quasi-scientific elements may have appealed to this impulse in Augustine. However, looking back, he identifies astrology as contrary to Christian belief, because it denies individual freedom of choice. If the stars really control human behavior, human beings are not responsible for their own sins. This line of reasoning makes God the creator of sin, rather than making human beings responsible for their own sinful choices. Such an outcome both denies God's supreme goodness and devalues human moral responsibility. This point is worth remembering whenever you are tempted to accuse Augustine of devaluing the human will when he insists on the absolute human dependence upon God's grace for salvation.

Literary Device

A distinguished friend advises Augustine that astrology is fake; its so-called predictions of the future based on mere chance. This man had studied astrology in his youth, but gave it up once he concluded that it was simply bogus. The friend's appearance in the narrative parallels that of an ex-Manichee bishop at the end of Book 3, who advises Monica that Augustine will give up Manichaeism after he discovers for himself that it is false. Augustine presents here a repeated pattern of messages from God that he repeatedly ignores; the messages are correct, but he did not heed them at the time. Astrology reappears in Book 7.6, where Augustine finally gives it up completely. Augustine's nameless female companion appears for the first time in Book 4. Scholars usually refer to her as his concubine, but their relationship was more like that of a modern common-law marriage or domestic partnership. Although they were never officially married, they stayed together for 15 years, and Augustine himself says that he was faithful to her during that time. They had one child, a son, whose conception Augustine describes as unwanted; procreation was one of the worst sins possible for Manichee. Augustine does not say that he loved his concubine, and he describes their relationship as one based solely on sex—a selfish desire—rather than on the kind of friendship that would include unselfish, spiritual love. Nonetheless, his reaction at her forced departure in Book 6.15 indicates that he did care for her in some way, and his relationship with their son, Adeodatus, was affectionate, as described in Book 9.

Augustine's attitudes toward women in the *Confessions* are easily open to criticism by modern readers. It is tempting to simplify them into the woman-as-saint (Monica) and woman-as-temptress (concubine) pattern, but simplification is not entirely fair. Monica manages to emerge as a strong and morally complex character, and even the unnamed concubine shows a greater moral resolve than Augustine is able to when she vows to live in chastity after she is forced to leave Augustine. Feminine imagery is also common in Augustine's language for his relationship with God. An example appears in Book 4.1, where Augustine describes himself as a child seeking nourishment at the breast of a motherly God. As for Augustine's assertion that there was no true friendship between him and his concubine, it is worth remembering that in Augustine's society, educated women were rare. For a brilliant and highly educated man like Augustine, true companionship would have required an intellectual aspect that would have been difficult to find with most women of his time. Spiritual friendship of this kind would have been restricted to his close male friends, one of whom, Nebridius, makes his first appearance at the end of this section.

Book 4, Chapters 4–13

Summary

A close friend of Augustine's, whom he had persuaded to become a Manichee, falls seriously ill, and while he is unconscious, his family has him baptized. He seems to recover, and Augustine jokes with him about the baptism, but his friend will not listen to his jokes. When his friend suddenly dies, Augustine is overcome with grief. Augustine eventually has to leave Thagaste for Carthage to escape the memories. The love of friends is good, but friends must be loved in God, not for themselves alone, for only God does not perish or change. People look for rest in the physical world and fix their hearts on things that pass away, not moving through them to recognition of the God who made them. True life and true love are found in Christ alone.

Commentary

Augustine's passionate attachment to his friends serves as the basis of this section, which discusses the nature of friendship. The death of Augustine's childhood friend in Thagaste acts as another message from God. His friend's Catholic family has him baptized on his deathbed, just as was almost done to Augustine. Now a Manichee, Augustine no longer believes baptism is necessary, but his friend, also a Manichee, abruptly refuses to share in his contempt for Catholic ritual and rejects Augustine's attention. Whether the baptism has a miraculous effect on his friend or his friend simply had a deathbed conversion is not made clear. Augustine is shaken by his friend's conversion but still refuses to see the message God is sending.

Augustine's description of his grief is familiar to anyone who has experienced the death of a loved one. But Augustine's excessive grief becomes a sin. He revels in his own misery, weeping inconsolably over his friend. Characteristically, Augustine turns to analysis of his emotions: Why, he asks, do tears give relief? He cannot answer this question, but analysis of the emotion of grief is a subject to which he returns in Book 9.12, where he weeps over Monica's death. Here, he condemns his grief as misplaced. His misery is a selfish indulgence; he makes clear that he cared more about his own grief than he cared about the welfare of his friend.

Theme

If Augustine's grief is misplaced, it is because his love is also misplaced. Augustine does not condemn the emotion of friendship. Indeed, his description of the simple pleasures of friendship in Book 4.8 is eloquent and moving. Augustine's error lies in treating his friend as an ultimate good, as an end unto himself. In his book *On Christian Doctrine,* Augustine makes an explicit distinction between things that are used as means to an end and things that are enjoyed for their own sake. All temporal things are objects of use; God alone should be the object of enjoyment. Even good and beautiful things, like the love of friends, can become stumbling blocks if people set them up as substitutes for the God who is their ultimate source. All human loves pass away, and people err in loving friends as substitutes for God, who alone is eternal and unchangeable. Human perception, limited by sin to the physical realm, can see only isolated pieces of the whole, but if you could grasp the whole as it really is, you would not want to linger in the transitory present. Augustine concludes this section with an invocation of praise to Christ, who was human but conquered death, whose love is unfailing, and who is the only true source of rest and peace.

Glossary

Orestes and Pylades   characters from Greek literature, famous for their devoted friendship.

Book 4, Chapters 13–16

Summary

At this time, Augustine still does not understand beauty; seeking to explain it, he writes a work *On the Beautiful and the Fitting,* which he has since lost. He dedicates it to a famous orator, whom he admired and wants to imitate. Augustine considers the nature of fame: He does not want empty celebrity, like actors and gladiators have, but something more serious. Augustine knows nothing about the man except what others said about him, yet he wants the man to admire his own work. Augustine remarks that he should show less intelligence and greater faith.

Commentary

Augustine wrote his book *De pulchro et apto (On the Beautiful and the Fitting)* in about the year 380, when he was 26 or 27 years old. The book has not survived, but by Augustine's report, it appears to have been an early, misguided attempt at describing the Platonic ascent that he later grasps fully in Book 7. Augustine claims not to remember much about it, except that it showed him still mired in a literal, physical understanding of the universe and of God. It also shows that he was already familiar with the ideas of the Neo-Platonists, because he uses the terms "Monad" and "Dyad." Although these were Platonic concepts, Neo-Platonism was not necessarily incompatible with Manichean beliefs, particularly in its insistence that evil has its origins in physical matter, with an existence separate from an immaterial God. Augustine also reports that he read Aristotle's *Categories,* which sought to classify the physical world, although the famous book did him no good, because it was still grounded in explanations of the physical.

Augustine's observations on fame may be of interest to readers in a modern, media-saturated society. Augustine comments that he actually knows nothing about the orator he admires so much, apart from the report of other people, who also know nothing in particular about him. If the gossip about the orator had been negative, Augustine would never have thought of him, although the man himself may have been just as talented as Augustine supposed. Augustine's vanity and desire for approval manifests itself here: Although he has never met the man, he is eager to attract the man's attention and approval. But Augustine wants "serious" fame for himself, not the kind of "low" celebrity that actors and gladiators (the star athletes of his time) possess, despite the fact that he admires these same celebrities himself. Once again, the irrational contradictions of Augustine's misdirected loves are on display.

Despite his avowals of his own unworthiness, Augustine does seem to allow himself a few moments of intellectual vanity in his description of how intelligent he is and how easily he masters a book like the *Categories,* which was famously difficult. Augustine's larger point, however, is that such books are not so magnificent as their worldly fame would lead people to believe, and that intelligence without faith is not as admirable as faith without intelligence. Augustine revisits this point in the opening chapters of Book 5.

Glossary

Monad and Dyad   Neo-Platonic philosophy had a triadic conception of the divine being. The Monad, or One, is transcendent and ineffable. There are two emanations from the Monad: the Dyad (or Intelligence) and the World-Soul. In the Dyad, the perfect unity of the One becomes divided to Ideas, and the World-Soul expresses these Ideas as physical Forms. In his discussion, Augustine indicates that he was identifying the Monad with the "good" God of Manichaeism, and the Dyad with the Manichaean concept of evil as a substance.

Book 5, Chapters 1–7

Summary

At 29, Augustine meets a Manichean bishop named Faustus, who is famous for his knowledge of doctrine. Augustine hopes Faustus can clear up some of his doubts regarding Manichean explanations of astronomy, which Augustine is starting to find improbable. The explanations of pagan scientists, although lacking in knowledge of Christ, are still more rationally consistent than those of the Manichees. Upon meeting Faustus, Augustine finds him pleasant and well-spoken, but no more knowledgeable than Augustine himself. Consequently, Augustine becomes disillusioned with Manichaeism, although he does not abandon it, because he still has found nothing better to replace it.

Commentary

Having been a Manichee for about nine years, Augustine is gradually losing faith in his chosen religion. Most importantly, the complex Manichean myths about the sun, moon, and stars have begun to strike Augustine as logically inconsistent and incompatible with the rational observations of science. Augustine's acceptance of the scientific knowledge of the pagan philosophers may seem strange at first glance. Augustine is careful to point out that scientific knowledge without knowledge of Christ is inadequate, but this idea in itself does not make scientific observation incorrect or worthless. For Augustine, the natural order is created by God to reflect divine order, and the ordered qualities of the physical world are accessible to human reason. Therefore, pagan astronomers can make valid observations about the natural order, predicting eclipses and plotting the courses of the stars, even if they do not have knowledge of God. However, amplifying a point he makes at the end of Book 4, Augustine asserts that simple faith, even without scientific knowledge, is better than scientific knowledge without faith. Augustine is always consistent in his assertion that knowledge of the created world, whether scientific or otherwise, is only good insofar as it leads upward, toward knowledge of the creator. However, Augustine also manages a note of criticism for those Christians who ignorantly assert incorrect beliefs about natural science.

Faustus, promised as someone who can answer Augustine's questions, turns out to be a disappointment. Faustus speaks agreeably and has a natural charm, but amidst the beautiful words, there is still no substance to satisfy Augustine's soul. Disillusioned, Augustine loses all enthusiasm for Manichaeism, but seeing no better alternatives, he does not make a break with it yet.

In the midst of this discussion, Augustine pauses to answer an objection that came from within the Catholic Christian community itself: the idea that truth cannot be expressed in elegant and polished language. Many Christians were deeply suspicious of the pagan traditions of education and rhetorical training that formed Augustine intellectually and whose failings he knew so well. Typically, Augustine avoids the simplistic answer. Beautiful expressions do not make something true, but neither do beautiful expressions make something false. Augustine explores the issue of a "Christian style" more fully in *On Christian Doctrine*. Augustine was deeply critical of traditional pagan education, but he also did much to rehabilitate pagan writers for Christian audiences by employing the metaphor of the "gold of the Egyptians." Just as the Israelites were allowed by God to plunder the gold of their Egyptian captors when they left slavery, so, too, are Christians allowed to make use of the wisdom of pagan writers, wherever such wisdom does not contradict revealed Christian truth.

Glossary

Faustus   c.340–390(?), Manichee bishop. At about the same time he was writing the *Confessions*, Augustine was also working on the *Contra Faustum Manicheum*, a detailed refutation of the Manichee preacher's teaching.

Great Bear   Ursa Major, the constellation of the Big Dipper.

Way, Word, Only-Begotten   names for Christ used in the New Testament.

Book 5, Chapters 8–14

Summary

At the urging of friends, Augustine leaves Carthage to teach in Rome, hoping to find a better-behaved group of students. Monica is violently opposed, and Augustine has to lie to her in order to get away from Carthage. At Rome, he falls ill and is on the verge of death. Although Monica does not know he is ill, God hears her constant prayers and prevents Augustine from dying while still a heretic. Augustine is growing steadily more skeptical about Manichaeism, feeling that the Academics, who doubt everything, may have the right idea. He still cannot believe Catholicism, because he can envision God and evil only as physical bodies, and he cannot answer Manichee criticisms of the Bible. To his disappointment, he soon discovers that Roman students are even worse than those he had in Carthage.

With the help of Manichee patrons, Augustine is appointed teacher of rhetoric in Milan, where he hears the sermons of Bishop Ambrose. At first, he is interested only in Ambrose's style, but he soon discovers that Ambrose applies a figurative interpretation to the Bible that allows him to defend against Manichee criticism. Augustine is still not completely convinced of the validity of Catholicism, but he decides to return to the Catholic Church for the time being.

Commentary

Now a successful rhetor, Augustine is nonetheless unhappy, professionally as well as spiritually. The disruptive students of Carthage, the Wreckers he had tried to avoid in his own student days, are making his life as a teacher miserable. Manichee friends promise him that the students in Rome are better behaved, and he will have greater opportunities for advancement there.

Monica is so opposed to Augustine's leaving that she insists on going with him, and Augustine resorts to blatant trickery to keep her from boarding the boat he leaves on. The *Confessions* are full of water imagery, and this passage contains a particularly lovely example: The sea-water Augustine travels is linked with the water of baptism that later washes him clean, and with Monica's rivers of tears for her son.

Literary Device

Augustine describes Monica's love for him as extreme, even excessive, and her sorrows are a deserved punishment for that excess. Although Monica has faith, she does not understand, any more than Augustine does at that time, that God is using Augustine's departure for a good end, so she protests what she cannot comprehend. Her attention is focused on herself, on the loss of the child she loves and the pain he causes her. Augustine points up the selfish nature of this love by referring to the "remnants of Eve" evident in Monica's behavior. Many scholars have noted the parallels between Augustine's desertion of Monica and Aeneas' desertion of Dido, mentioned in Book 3. In the *Aeneid,* Aeneas must leave Dido because her love threatens to distract him from his destiny; so, too, does Monica's love threaten to impede Augustine on his spiritual journey.

If his spiritual ties to Manichaeism are weakening, Augustine is still socially tied to the Manichee community—in fact, he is living with Manichee friends during his illness, and Manichee patrons arrange for his job in Rome. He remains preoccupied by the question of evil. The Manichees taught that evil or sin was distinct physical entity, alien to humankind, so that all human sin could be said to come from outside the human will. In Augustine's later estimation, this belief appeals to his vanity, because it allows him to excuse himself from responsibility for any wrong he committed by blaming a cause outside himself.

Disillusioned, Augustine becomes attracted by the radical skepticism of the Academics, a group of philosophers who held that absolute knowledge of the truth was impossible for human beings. His attraction to skepticism proceeds from a kind of despair: Although he feels doubt about Manichaeism, he also feels doubt about Catholicism. Nothing he has believed now seems secure or reliable. Augustine still cannot wrap his mind around anything except a material notion of good and evil; he thinks of them as things having mass, existing in space. At the same time, he cannot believe in the Incarnation of Christ. Catholicism holds that Christ was born from a human woman, the Virgin Mary; had a real human body; and was fully human as well as fully divine. Manichaeism, which believed the body to be evil and corrupt, could not accept that Christ had ever had actual flesh; instead, he was a being of pure light and merely projected the illusion of a body for the sake of his followers.

Augustine probably arrived in Milan in late 384, at the age of 30. Milan was a major center of power; the Roman Emperors kept court in Milan because Rome was becoming increasingly unsafe, threatened by barbarian armies. The formidable Bishop of Milan, Ambrose, was later declared a saint and a Doctor (or fundamental thinker) of the Catholic Church, just as Augustine himself later was. Ambrose was famous for his eloquent sermons. For the first time, Augustine finds not only beautiful words—he describes Ambrose's language as charming—but content, the substance he has been looking for. In this respect, Ambrose contrasts Faustus in Book 5, who has nothing beyond linguistic polish and a little personal charm to offer Augustine. Ambrose has been strongly influenced by the Neo-Platonists, and he applies a Platonistic, spiritual interpretation to the Christian texts he expounds for his congregation. In doing so, he frees Augustine, for the first time, from the literal interpretation of scripture that the Manichees relied on. Understood figuratively, the Bible suddenly begins to sound intellectually and morally defensible to Augustine. Ambrose's influence moves Augustine to make a distinct, although somewhat half-hearted, break with the Manichees. For the Augustine who looks back at his life, this turn of events is entirely providential: God has led him to Milan for the purpose of encountering Ambrose, so that he can begin his return to the true faith.

Glossary

Cyprian   Bishop of Carthage and martyr, d. 258. He was a kind of patron saint for North Africa and the subject of intense popular devotion.

Elpidius   nothing is known of Elpidius beyond what Augustine says.

Symmachus   c.345–402. Roman prefect, aristocrat, and pagan. Symmachus had a reputation for promoting talent, but he also had reasons for recommending Augustine, a non-Catholic, to a public post in Milan. Just prior to Augustine's appointment, Symmachus had asked the Emperor in Milan to reinstate toleration of pagan rites, a request that Ambrose had managed to block.

Book 6, Chapters 1–10

Summary

Monica has come to join Augustine in Milan. She is pleased, but not surprised, to hear that Augustine has given up Manichaeism. When Bishop Ambrose forbids her from making offerings for the dead, as was customary in Africa, she obediently gives up the practice. Augustine admires Ambrose and is eager to speak with him, but Ambrose is always busy. Augustine is beginning to understand that in his intellectual pride, he completely misinterpreted the ideas of the Catholic Church. He is still driven by ambition and pride, and he worries about his career. He sees a beggar in the street and is dismayed to think that the beggar is happier than he is.

Augustine discusses his friends Alypius and Nebridius, who had joined Manichaeism because of him and were with him in Milan. In Carthage, Alypius had a weakness for the circus games, which he gave up immediately after a rebuke from Augustine. But in Milan, he is seduced by the gladiatorial shows, against his better judgment. He is mistakenly accused of crime he did not commit, and only God's intervention saves him, in the form of a witness to his good character. Alypius earned his reputation for integrity as a junior lawyer by resisting the bribes and threats of a powerful senator. Like Alypius, Nebridius is also a dear friend to Augustine, a Manichee, and a brilliant thinker. The three of them look for truth together.

Commentary

Theme

Book 6 is distinguished by several digressions from the narrative of Augustine's life into the lives of those around him, most notably Monica and his friend Alypius. A parallel theme in the stories concerns giving up a bad habit after being corrected by a wise friend. Monica, who has already earned a reputation for piety in Milan, is following the traditions of her homeland by bringing offerings of food and wine to the tombs of martyred saints. Although Monica herself is absolutely sober and respectful, Ambrose has forbidden the practice because of its tendency to be misused as an occasion for wild parties and its similarity to pagan rites. Somewhat to Augustine's surprise, Monica gives it up without complaint after she hears Ambrose's order. Monica's story also emphasizes one of Augustine's recurring themes: the abandonment of the physical for the high good of the spiritual. Instead of food, Monica learns to bring her heartfelt prayers to honor the saints. Like Monica, Alypius also gives up a bad habit, his addiction to circus games, after hearing a veiled rebuke on the subject during one of Augustine's lectures. Like Monica, he does not complain or take offense, but immediately changes his behavior. The circus games were violent public spectacles involving wild animals, and Alypius' weakness for them may be compared to Augustine's own weakness for the theater, in that both stir up negative emotions for no good purpose.

The behavior of Monica and Alypius contrasts with that of Augustine at this point in his life. Like them, he has heard a rebuke, at least in a figurative sense: He has discovered that Manichaeism is false, and he knows that he has misinterpreted Catholic doctrine. Unlike his companions, however, Augustine fails to change his bad habits. He is stuck, unable to go back to Manichaeism or fully embrace Catholicism, instead wavering about his beliefs and his plans. The force of simple habit in encouraging sinful behavior is a recurring theme in Augustine's works. In fact, even Alypius does not escape it entirely. After he arrives, he is cajoled by a group of friends into going to the gladiatorial games, another extremely violent and bloody public entertainment. Thinking himself strong enough to resist the temptation, he sneaks a peek at the action and is once again hooked, despite his best intentions. Sin is not so easily conquered by the simple force of human will. The same kind of peer pressure that operated on Augustine's theft of pears in Book 2 also operates on Alypius, as his group of friends carries him along to a sin he would never have committed alone.

Alypius also appears in what can only be called a comic interlude. In a plot that reads like something out of a stock melodrama, he is accused of a crime after he is discovered innocently examining the axe that a thief discarded while being pursued. In some respects, the little collection of tales about Alypius has the tone of a hagiography, the legend of a saint's life. Exactly why it appears here in such detail is not completely clear. Alypius was alive at the time Augustine was writing, was still a close friend, and was the bishop of Thagaste, their childhood home. The scholar Pierre Courcelle theorized that Augustine had intended to write a biography of Alypius, and Book 6 gives the remnants of that biography. Most critics are skeptical of this theory, but convincing explanations are hard to find. Alypius' prominent appearance may simply reflect the fact that Paulinus of Nola's request for information about Alypius' life and Augustine's life—a request originally sent to Alypius—helped encourage Augustine to write the *Confessions*. In a literary sense, the good Alypius, who is chaste and honest, does act within the narrative as a contrast to Augustine's portrait of his own bad character. Perhaps, finally, Augustine simply wanted to pay a compliment to an old friend. Interestingly, the tale of Alypius' close call is not the only comic touch in this section. Augustine slips in an affectionate dig about Monica when he mentions that Nebridius also left his father and mother—a mother who did not follow him all the way to Milan.

The final important character in this section is Ambrose, seen from afar through young Augustine's eyes. For Augustine the bishop, Ambrose must have served as a role model, and Augustine's description of the many demands on Ambrose's time has the plaintive ring of personal experience. Augustine never gets to question Ambrose alone, as he did with Faustus in Book 5. Augustine had hoped Faustus could privately give him secret answers; with Ambrose, all the answers are out in the open, in his public sermons and in the Christian scriptures that anyone is free to study. When not preaching or ministering to his congregation, Ambrose reads silently. While silent reading was not necessarily unusual, it was common in the Classical world to read aloud, particularly if the reader was not alone. Ambrose's concentrated silence is the opposite of the "loquaciousness" of the Manichees, who use their pretty words for deceit, just as Augustine the rhetor does. Rather than talking, Ambrose is listening to the word of God, something Augustine has as yet not done.

Glossary

assessor   a person acting as a consultant or advisor in matters of law.

Book 6, Chapters 7–16

Summary

Now 30, Augustine is dismayed by his own indecision. He is still ambitious for worldly success, and he cannot imagine giving up sex for a life of religious celibacy. Monica arranges for him to marry a Christian girl from a good family, but she is too young, so the marriage is postponed two years. Augustine and his friends talk about withdrawing from the world to take up a life of philosophical contemplation, but the plan falls apart when they realize their wives will not approve. Augustine sends away his concubine in preparation for the marriage, and her loss causes him great pain. But he cannot bear the thought of two years without sex, so he finds another woman. His only solace is the conversation of his friends, and friendship forms the one pure bond in his life.

Commentary

Style &
Language

The latter half of Book 6 opens with a marvelously ironic summary of the events leading up to Augustine's current situation and his mental state at that point in life. Augustine speaks in a kind of internal monologue, restlessly hopping from one source of enlightenment to the next—Faustus, the Academics, Ambrose—and constantly asking anxious questions that never quite get answered: "How will I find the right books to give me the answers I want, and even if I ever find them, when will I get time to read them?" The tone is one of self-mockery, and it contributes to the oddly comic feel of Book 6. A further comic touch occurs later in this section: Augustine's group hatches a high-minded plan to withdraw from the world and do nothing but contemplate philosophical questions, but the idea instantly collapses when the real world interrupts: Their wives will never let them do it!

Worldly concerns are pressing hard on Augustine. Always fond of triads, Augustine identifies his three worldly temptations: honors, money, and marriage. He has already established a highly successful career: He has secured a plum government position, won prizes for his orations, delivered tributes for the emperor, and attracted the attention of powerful men. He and his friends are doing so well, in fact, that they are beginning to contemplate how they can become the governors of minor provinces, not an impossibility provided that they can prevail on their network of influential friends and they can marry into enough money.

Marrying into money appears to be exactly what Monica arranges for him. As Augustine presents it, Monica's motivations are relatively pure: She wants to see him legitimately married into a good Catholic family, hoping that he will then be baptized. However, the fact that Monica has followed Augustine to Milan—most likely with at least one of his brothers (Navigius, who appears later in the narrative) and possibly two cousins—seems to indicate exactly how much the entire family has pinned its hopes on Augustine's success and social status. The marriage Monica contracts for Augustine is purely a social arrangement, not a love match. The girl herself is two years below the legal age for marriage, which makes her 10 years old, while Augustine is 30, but the wide difference in age was common in contracted marriages. Dreams again play a role: Monica has dreams and visions about the marriage, but she knows that this time they are false, generated by her own desires rather than by genuine communication from God. Nonetheless, she continues with the plan.

One consequence is that Augustine's concubine has to be disposed of. She is sent back home to Africa, although their son, Adeodatus, stays with Augustine. Many writers have pointed out that despite the pathos of the scene, it is a reflection of the social realities of the time. No one in Augustine's social circles would have considered his concubine marriageable. Concubinage was a legal gray area, one made necessary by the rigid class system of late Roman society, in which marriage was an alliance between families and estates, not an affair based on personal preferences. It was inevitable that at some point, Augustine, the successful rhetor, would be expected to contract a legally sanctioned marriage with a bride from a respectable family. These facts are important to understanding Augustine's world. However, they do not adequately account for the way that Augustine reports on the event. Augustine describes it without sugarcoating the facts or attempting to excuse his behavior. He makes quite clear that he is abandoning his partner in a faithful relationship of 15 years, the mother of his son, strictly because she has become an obstacle to his success. Throughout the passage, Augustine is careful to put all the blame on his side. His mistress, in fact, comes away with the moral high ground, because she vows to live a life of religious celibacy, something Augustine acknowledges he could not do. Augustine's behavior grows worse: Although he grieves for the loss of his concubine, he cannot imagine going without sex for two years, so he takes another lover for the interim. The event is reported as yet another of Augustine's blameworthy actions, the product of his ambition, his concupiscence, and his willing involvement in the hollow values of his society.

Character Insight

The immediate contrast to the repudiation of his concubine is Augustine's devotion to his friends, the one pure and blameless aspect of his life. He acknowledges that he could not recognize it at the time, but he could never have been happy without the companionship of his friends, who were still accompanying him on his painful search for truth. This pure friendship is the opposite of the selfish physical lust that mars Augustine's relationships with his concubine and his temporary lover.

Glossary

Epicurus   c. 341–270 B.C. Greek philosopher who held that the ultimate good was to feel pleasure and avoid pain. Epicurus made a famous argument concerning God and evil, to which Augustine may be alluding: "Is God willing to prevent evil, but not able? Then he is not omnipotent. Is he able, but not willing? Then he is malevolent. Is he both able and willing? Then where does evil come from? Is he neither able nor willing? Then why call him God?"

Book 7, Chapters 1–21

Summary

Augustine describes his attempts to think about the nature of God. He still conceives of God as a kind of matter, like air or water, filling the spaces of the universe. Nebridius has already proposed a convincing argument against the dualist mythology of the Manichees: If God can be harmed by evil, then God is not all-powerful, which is absurd; if God cannot be harmed by evil, why is there any need for God to fight evil? But Augustine is still troubled by the origin of evil, which he cannot comprehend because he still does not comprehend Christ. He begins to understand that sin results from the corruption of the human will. He is finally convinced that astrology is false, after he hears the story of a rich man and a beggar born at exactly the same moment, so that their horoscopes must be the same. Then he reads the works of the Platonists, and he sees Christ reflected in them. Using Platonic ideas, he is finally able to move upward through material things to the contemplation of the immaterial divine. Augustine comprehends that to God, there is no evil; seen as a totality, from the perspective of God's eternity, the entire creation is harmonious and good. Sin is a rejection of the higher good, God, for the lower goods of material things. Contemplation of these truths is too much for Augustine's strength, but by the mediation of Christ between the material and immaterial, understanding is possible. Having read the Platonists, Augustine is now able to study the Bible with a clearer understanding, because Platonism alone is not enough to save him.

Commentary

Book 7 is one of the most tightly constructed sections of the *Confessions*, in which Augustine describes in detail how he finally comes to understand God, Christ, and evil. As the middle book of the 13 in the *Confessions*, Book 7 marks the decisive turning point in Augustine's thought. Only one piece of narrative interrupts the dense description of Augustine's intellectual processes: the story of the slave child and the rich child born at the same moment, which finally convinces Augustine that astrology is phony. For many readers, this story seems out of place, so much so that some scholars have argued it was a later addition to the original text, but it does have possible ties to the rest of Book 7. Rejection of astrology relates to the question of free will. Augustine has already stated in Book 4.3 that astrology denies the freedom of the will, and Augustine's realization in Book 7 that sin is a perversion of the human will forms another part of his rejection of Manichaeism.

The key to Augustine's intellectual prison comes in the form of "some books of the Platonists." No one knows the identity of the man "puffed up with pride" who gave Augustine these books or even what books they were, although scholars find strong echoes of the writings of Plotinus and Porphyry in Book 7. Interestingly, Augustine begins his discussion of the Platonic books by quoting from the opening of the gospel of John: "In the beginning was the Word..." The Platonic books contain these same notions, Augustine insists, even if they do not mention Christ, the Word. Augustine is exploiting the "gold of the Egyptians"—taking whatever is useful from pagan philosophy without accepting all of pagan philosophy's ideas.

Platonism supplies Augustine with a theoretical framework that allows him to think of a God who has no physical substance. Unlike the ineffectual, physically limited Manichee deity, the Platonic divinity is eternal, infinite, immanent, incorruptible, unchanging, and perfect. The immaterial Platonic god represents a consummate good that is imperfectly glimpsed in the material world. In 7.17, Augustine offers a classic formulation of the "Platonic ascent" that leads from the material to the immaterial: from the physical body, to the soul, to the soul's inner power, to higher reasoning, to the source of higher reason. This is the beatific vision, in which the human mind has direct apprehension of the divine, but Augustine cannot sustain it for long, being pulled downward by his material body—specifically, by his sexual impulses. The beatific vision supplies Augustine with a radical solution for the problem of evil. Seen from God's perspective, outside of time, comprehending the entire universe, there is no evil; evil is nothing, having no existence of its own. It occurs only as a corruption of things that are good.

What the Platonic books do not offer Augustine is any notion of Christ's Incarnation as a human being or his death on the cross. The importance of Christ as a mediator between human and God, material and spiritual, is a key point for Augustine. Augustine must supplement his reading with Christian scripture, and especially with the letters of St. Paul, recorded in the New Testament. These letters are of primary importance in Book 8, when a passage from one of them finally clinches

Augustine's emotional conversion. Christology occupies much of the last half of Book 7, where Augustine runs through the different heretical interpretations of Christ's nature. Augustine says that at the time, he held the Platonist's view that Christ was not divine simply a good and wise man, while Alypius shared the view of the Apollinarians that Christ was simply God poured into a human shape, not having a human soul or mind. Debates over the exact nature of Christ were rampant in the early church, having been resolved only in 325 by the Council of Nicea and the formulation of the Nicene Creed. Augustine finally affirms that view, that Christ was both fully God and fully human. For Augustine, Christ provides the only real resolution to the matter of human sin. In 7.5, the anxiety reflected in his restless flurry of questions about evil comes to rest only in a statement of faith in Christ, and when his mind is overwhelmed by the glory of the beatific vision in 7.17, his discussion in 7.18 turns to Christ, the only bridge between frail humanity and the transcendent glory of God.

Although Augustine's mistaken beliefs are now clear to him, this is not yet the end of his journey back to God. The intellectual process that has been at work since Book 4 finally culminates in Book 8, with Augustine's emotional acceptance of God's will.

Glossary

Vindicianus   the doctor who tries to warn Augustine against astrology in Book 4.5.

Firminus   nothing is known of Firminus beyond what Augustine says.

Jacob and Esau   twin sons of Isaac (see Genesis, 25 and 27).

Photinus   d. 376, condemned for heresy in 351. Photinus believed that Christ as the Son of God did not exist before the Incarnation; this belief was contrary to orthodox doctrine that the Son was eternal and uncreated.

Apollinarians   the Apollinarian heresy held that Christ had a human body but not a human spirit.

Book 8, Chapters 1–4

Summary

Augustine is now a Christian in his heart, but he is unable to give up his worldly affairs, particularly sex. He goes to speak with Simplicianus, Ambrose's teacher. Simplicianus congratulates him for studying the books of the Platonists and tells him the story of Victorinus. Victorinus was a distinguished rhetor in Rome, and for most of his life he was a vocal defender of paganism. In his old age, he accepted Christianity, but he was afraid to attend church or be baptized. Finally, he decided to be publicly baptized. Augustine observes that things lost are dearer when found again, and that the conversion of those who were previously opponents of the faith sets a great example for others.

Commentary

Augustine's internal conversion now must be matched by an external conversion. Augustine's way of thinking has changed, but he is still a man of the world, pursuing a high-powered career, planning to marry an heiress, and maintaining a lover on the side. Looking for advice, he meets with Simplicianus, Ambrose's mentor. Like Augustine, Simplicianus and Ambrose are both Christian Platonists. Simplicianus offers Augustine a lesson in the example of Marius Victorinus, the scholar who was responsible for translating Augustine's "books of the Platonists" into Latin. Victorinus' career mirrored Augustine's: He was a successful rhetor and a prominent enemy of Christianity before his conversion.

Literary Device

Not surprisingly, Augustine sees his own situation in this story. He adds to it New Testament examples of the return of the lost, referring to a housewife's lost coin, the good shepherd who finds his lost lamb, and the return of the Prodigal Son, whose story forms a kind of framework for the *Confessions*. Augustine's other prominent model of conversion, Saint Paul the Apostle, also makes an appearance in this section. Like Augustine and Victorinus, Paul was a prominent opponent of Christianity before becoming its advocate. Augustine observes that such public examples of conversion lead others to salvation. For Augustine, this has a double significance: His own example will be first in his public acceptance of baptism and second in the writing of the *Confessions* itself.

Public affirmation of the Christian religion is difficult enough for Augustine, but with typical ambition, he has raised the bar for himself to its ultimate height. As he points out, anticipating his readers' objections, it would have been perfectly acceptable for him to join the church but to remain in public life and to marry. But Augustine cannot be satisfied with anything less than a total commitment to his new faith: withdrawal from the world, his career, his honors, and most painfully, from all sexual activity. In a sense, this commitment substitutes one kind of ambition for another: Formerly driven to excel in the world, Augustine is now driven to excel in his faith. Characteristically, Augustine cannot do anything by halves, and his painful deliberations over this radical change in his life are about to reach a crisis point. His return home to God is imminent, and he quotes the story of the Prodigal Son twice in 8.3, referring to the one who was dead, but is now alive.

Glossary

Simplicianus d. c.400. Ambrose's spiritual father; succeeded Ambrose as bishop of Milan in 397.

pearl in Christ's parable of the "Pearl of Great Price," (Matthew 13:45–46) a merchant finds a precious pearl and then sells everything that he has in order to buy it.

Anubis, Neptune, Venus, Minerva Anubis was an Egyptian god of the underworld. Neptune, Venus, and Minerva were the Roman gods of the sea, love, and wisdom, respectively. The line is quoted from the *Aeneid.* The point was that the Romans had become devoted to cults imported from Egypt, a conquered Roman territory.

old leaven (or yeast) a reference to I Corinthians 5:7–8: "Christ our Passover has been sacrificed for us. Therefore let us keep the feast; not with the old leaven, neither with the leaven of malice and wickedness, but with the unleavened bread of sincerity and truth."

Book 8, Chapters 5–12

Summary

Augustine is moved by the story of Victorinus, but his old life has become a habit he cannot break. He is deeply distressed, therefore, that he cannot leave his old life now that he no longer has any doubts about Christianity. Augustine and Alypius are visited by Ponticianus, who tells them about St. Antony. Ponticianus then tells them about two of his friends who were inspired to dedicate their lives to Christ after reading the story of St. Antony. Augustine is overcome with shame at his inability to follow their example. Extremely agitated, Augustine retreats to the garden of their house. His will is divided, but Augustine observes that both contrary wills were his own, not a good will and a bad will, as the Manichees believe. Augustine breaks down in tears beneath a fig tree. He hears a voice saying, "Take and read." Interpreting this as a message from God, he picks up his copy of the letters of St. Paul and reads a passage that puts his mind at rest. He resolves to dedicate his entire life to God, and Alypius joins him in this resolve.

Commentary

Augustine's final conversion at the end of Book 8 is the most famous episode from the *Confessions*. In a moment of intense emotional crisis, Augustine hears a mysterious child's voice chanting, "Take and read, take and read." When he does so, he encounters Romans 13:13–14, and the passage abruptly lays to rest all his doubts and fears about leaving his old life behind. In a way, it is almost a fairy-tale ending: Augustine has been desperately looking for certainty his entire spiritual life, and here, in one moment of clarity, he gets the relief that only absolute certainty can give him. Intellectually, he has been prepared for this moment for some time, and emotionally, he has been in a state of steadily growing anxiety. The "take and read" episode is the catalyst for decisive change in Augustine's life. (Incidentally, readers puzzled by Augustine's insistence on a life of complete continence need only look at the other examples in this chapter and Chapter 9 for a cultural context: The fiancées of two converted men immediately join them in dedicating their virginity to God; Verecundus is disappointed that he cannot withdraw from the world because he is married; and Alypius shows his self-denial by walking around barefoot all winter.)

The conversion episode is foreshadowed in Book 8 by two stories that mirror Augustine's experience. The story of Victorinus, the converted rhetor, appears in the first part of Book 8, although you are not certain from Augustine's description how much time separates his hearing of that story from his conversion experience. The second story, the one about Ponticianus' friends, immediately precedes the conversion episode. A third story, that of St. Antony of the Desert, provides the backdrop for the conversion of Ponticianus' friend and of Augustine, although Augustine does not supply the details for his readers. In a culture that valued asceticism, Antony was an exemplary model of self-denial. After reading Christ's exhortation to "sell all you have" in Matthew 19:21, Antony sold all of his family's estate, gave the proceeds to the poor, and retired to the desert as a hermit, eating little and praying constantly. God allowed Satan to tempt Antony in several visions, but Antony withstood all temptations. Antony's example of personal purity and withdrawal from the world has obvious connections to Augustine's situation. Furthermore, both Antony and Ponticianus' unnamed friends are moved to give up the world after reading a crucial passage, just as Augustine finally is. Echoes of Book 6, with its themes of giving up bad habits after hearing pertinent advice from a wise friend, are also apparent, both here and in the story of Victorinus, who was moved to convert publicly on the advice of Simplicianus. Habit is the force that ties Augustine to his worldly life of sins, even when he wants to try to leave it, and Augustine specifically associates this force of habit with the idea of original sin, inherited from Adam.

Biblical echoes also inform Augustine's description. Along with the parallels between this scene of Augustine's grief beneath the fig tree and his theft from the pear tree in Book 3, both of these have connections to the story of the Fall in the Garden of Eden. One Christian tradition held that a fig tree, rather than an apple, was the tree from which Adam and Eve ate, and the fact that they used fig leaves to cover their nakedness after the Fall contributed to making the fig a symbol of carnal lust. The fig tree has further echoes in the New Testament, where it has special significance as a symbol of faith without acts. Christ tells the parable of the fig tree that does not bear fruit and so is cut down and burned (Luke 13:6–9), and Christ curses the fig tree that has leaves but no fruit (Matthew 21:19). Finally, Christ calls his disciple Nathaniel from under the fig tree (John 3:48–50). Augustine's intense physical and emotional distress in his garden also recalls Christ's agony in the garden of Gethsemane (Matthew 26:36–45), which precedes his crucifixion.

Style & Language

From a narrative standpoint, Augustine saps some of the drama from his conversion narrative by inserting a long digression about the Manichees immediately prior the "take and read" event. Augustine is in the garden, in a state of intense physical and mental agitation, and then the garden seems to disappear as Augustine launches into an analysis of his divided will, taking the opportunity to point out errors of Manichee doctrine along the way. However, his discussion is relevant because it concerns the relationship between sin and the human will, introduced in Book 7. When Augustine reminds readers several paragraphs later that he is still in the garden, the transition is jarring.

Literary Device

Augustine also inserts into this section the appearance of Lady Continence. Some critics have insisted that Augustine is reporting an actual vision of the beautiful lady who beckons to him, but Augustine is simply using the literary device of personification. He amusingly represents his sins as annoying pests that hold him back and whisper doubts into his ears, while serene Continence and her followers encourage him onward to his new life.

With all of these symbolic, literary, and biblical connections, many modern readers have asked: Is Augustine's account of his conversion literally true? In some ways, this is not an entirely relevant question. Augustine presents the event through the lens of memory, accumulated experience, and literary art. If his account is stylized or laden with symbolic associations, it does not necessarily make it less true in a spiritual sense. Autobiography always presents the author's life events in hindsight, in the way that the author has come to understand them and wants the reader to interpret them. Under such circumstances, literal truth is no longer at issue.

Book 9, Chapters 1–7

Summary

Following his conversion, Augustine has decided not to withdraw from public life immediately, not wanting to appear vain. He decides to resign his teaching job after an upcoming vacation period, and a chest illness gives him a further excuse to retire. Verecundus is upset that he cannot withdraw from public life because he is married, but he dies not long afterward as a baptized Christian. Nebridius also is baptized soon after Augustine, and he, too, dies soon after. Before that time, however, the friends set out for Verecundus' country estate, where they spend the vacation period studying scripture and philosophy. When the vacation is over, Augustine notifies Ambrose that he wants to be baptized. Alypius joins him in baptism, as does Adeodatus, Augustine's son; Adeodatus dies a few years later. Discussing how much the music of the church moved him, Augustine explains how Ambrose resisted a siege by Empress Justina while the faithful chanted psalms.

Commentary

Book 9 opens with Augustine's delayed decision to withdraw from his former life and dedicate himself to Christianity. He has to defend himself against critics who charged that if his conversion had really been sincere, he would have left public life immediately. Here, Augustine offers a counter argument: He does not want to appear vain and self-important by making a great show of conversion. At the time, Augustine was also suffering from a chest problem that left him short of breath—a condition he considers a merciful gift from God to allow him to retire. Modern readers may be more likely to think that the severe emotional turmoil preceding his conversion affected Augustine's health.

Death is a prominent theme of Book 9. In the first half of Book 9, Augustine mentions the deaths of three members of his circle. All three deaths are presented anachronistically, interrupting the chronology of the narrative. Verecundus, his rich friend who owns the estate at Cassiciacum, is the first. Verecundus cannot join his friends in a life of celibacy because he is married. Modern readers may not share Augustine's belief that God rewarded Verecundus by allowing him to die soon thereafter, so that he was released from his worldly entanglements. The date of Nebridius' death is uncertain, but he died relatively young, was a cleric like Augustine, and evidently remained a close friend to Augustine until his death. Finally, Augustine mentions his son, Adeodatus, who dies about two years after Augustine's baptism. Augustine speaks of him as a fine boy, intelligent and thoughtful. Augustine reports all three deaths with an air of wistfulness, but not sorrow; he is confident that all three of his loved ones died in God's keeping. Narratively, the deaths prepare the reader for the longer discussion of Monica's death that occupies the last half of Book 9. All of the deaths emphasize the theme of change— the death of the old life and the beginning of the new—just as Augustine's life is so fundamentally altered by his conversion and baptism. Interestingly, the account of his actual baptism, at Easter 387 in Milan, slips by almost unnoticed, with no narrative fanfare. The degree to which Augustine has changed is illustrated by an important detail: Ambrose advises the newly converted Augustine to read from the book of Isaiah. Augustine tries, but cannot make sense of it. In Book 3.5, when confronted with much the same problem, he decides that the Bible is simply unworthy of study; now, he sets aside the book for a time when he will be better prepared to interpret its meaning.

Augustine's withdrawal to Verecundus' country estate at Cassiciacum with his circle of friends and family was an intellectually and spiritually fertile time, lasting from the fall of 386 to the spring of 387. Augustine wrote four works during this period: *Contra academicos* (Against the Academics), *De beata vita* (On the Happy Life), *De ordine* (On Order) and *Soliloquia* (Soliloquies). But Augustine's account here of his time at Cassiciacum consists mainly of an extended analysis of Psalm 4, describing his emotion at breaking the hold Manichee philosophy had over him.

Music was a continuing interest of Augustine's: He returns to it in Book 10, and he wrote a treatise on the subject, *De musica* (On Music). The use of music during worship was viewed with suspicion in the early church, but Milan was the birthplace of Ambrosian chant, a form of plainchant that remained popular throughout the Middle Ages. Ambrose wrote verses for his congregation to sing, one of which Augustine quotes near the end of Book 8. Augustine introduces the idea of singing psalms during times of distress via the story of Justina's siege of Ambrose's basilica. The event Augustine describes actually took place just before Easter of 386, well before Augustine had his conversion experience. Justina, the mother of the child-emperor Valentinian, was an adherent of Arianism, one of the many competing varieties of Christianity in Augustine's time. The Arians held the heretical belief that Christ, as the son of God, was lesser than God himself. Justina had issued an edict of toleration for Arianism and ordered Ambrose to hand over his church for Arian worship services. Ambrose refused, staging a sit-in by the Catholic faithful inside the basilica to prevent Justina's troops from confiscating it. Ambrose won the argument, as Justina was finally forced to withdraw. Augustine associates a miraculous element with this tale: Ambrose has a vision that leads to the discovery of the incorrupt bodies of two martyred saints, Protasius and Gervasius; their relics then cure a blind man. The significance of this tale at this point in Augustine's narrative is not immediately clear, and Augustine himself protests that he is not quite sure why he included it. However, the element of the miraculous appears elsewhere in Book 9, in the mysterious voice with its message to Augustine and in his toothache suddenly healed by the prayers of his friends. Furthermore, the triumph of the Catholic church over its heretical opponents relates to Augustine's internal triumph over Manichaeism.

Glossary

vintage vacation   a traditional Roman vacation period during harvest time, from late August to mid-October.

Book 9, Chapters 8–13

Summary

While Augustine's group is at the port of Ostia, Monica dies, Augustine reminisces about her. He describes her childhood and how she began sneaking wine from the cask when she was sent to fetch it; a servant cruelly taunted her about this habit, and she immediately gave it up. As a married woman, she was obedient to her husband and diplomatic in dealing with him. Her mother-in-law at first was hostile toward her, but Monica's patience and gentleness won her over. While Augustine and Monica were at Ostia, they talked one day about eternal life, and together they experienced a vision of that joy. When Monica was ill, she abandoned her former desire to be buried with her husband in Africa, because her true home was in God. Augustine is overwhelmed by grief at her loss, even though he knows that her death is a good event. He does not weep, even at her funeral, but later, he weeps for Monica, for which God will forgive him. Augustine asks God, through Christ, to forgive Monica's sins and asks the readers to remember his parents in prayer.

Commentary

Augustine's little group has decided to move back to Africa. War delays their departure, and the group is forced to wait at the port city of Ostia, at the mouth of the river Tiber, which is under a blockade. There, in late 387, Monica falls ill and dies. Augustine devotes the rest of Book 9 to an account of Monica's life. As in the story of his own life, Augustine selects only a few representative events from each stage of her life to demonstrate important aspects of Monica's character. He begins with her childhood and her habit of sipping wine from the cask. Patient teaching from her good nurse is not sufficient to cure her of her vice; only a hurtful insult from a slave changes her ways. The story echoes the earlier tales of Monica and Alypius, where a comment ends a bad habit, as well as Augustine's own conversion upon hearing a command from God. It also reflects one of Augustine's frequent observations, that God always turns pain to a good end, even if those who inflicted the pain had bad motives. Throughout his description, Augustine presents

Monica as an ideal model of feminine Christian virtue: obedient, humble, devout, peace-making, selflessly caring for others.

The account of Augustine and Monica's vision at Ostia is almost as famous as Augustine's actual conversion. The story has clear parallels to Augustine's mystical vision at the height of the Platonic ascent in Book 7. Discussing eternal life, the two experience the direct, unmediated contact of the higher human mind with the divine. In this immaterial realm, the physical senses receive no impressions, and the mind itself is silent. Language, which always stands in between the mind and the external world, obscuring understanding, is no longer necessary. This is the true reality, the eternal, perfect, and unchanging realm of God, which is the true home of all human souls. The scene is the preparation for Monica's departure: Having experienced this perfection and with her son reclaimed for the church, she has no more fear of death. Her sudden renunciation of her desire to be buried next to her husband in Thagaste testifies to the fact that her true home is with God; where her body lies is of no consequence.

Augustine also realizes that Monica's death is not an occasion for sorrow. Nonetheless, his pain at her passing is intense. In contrast to his behavior at the death of his close friend in Book 4, now Augustine tries to moderate his grief. But he is still human, and he finally does weep for her and for himself. In Book 4, he condemns his tears as selfish and misdirected. Now, he concludes that Christian love does not preclude tears of grief; God accepts such sorrows with compassion, even if philosophers may quibble about them.

Following Monica's death, Augustine was forced to return to Rome and wait another year before it was safe to sail back to Africa. However, the end of Book 9 marks the end of the narrative of Augustine's spiritual life. Having begun his story with praise, Augustine ends here with prayer and a reminder of the heavenly Jerusalem, the true home of all Christians, to which they hope to return from their life's wanderings.

Glossary

Evodius   Evodius appears as a speaker in two of Augustine's dialogues; he became bishop of Uzali in about the year 400, and continued to correspond with Augustine as late as 414.

my brother   Augustine's brother was named Navigius, and it is likely that he came to Milan with Monica.

Book 10, Chapters 1–25

Summary

Augustine asks to know God as well as God knows him. God knows Augustine's heart. Why then does Augustine confess before his readers? They cannot know Augustine's heart, but in Christian charity, they will know he tells the truth. By his example, his fellow believers will be moved to thank God and to change their own lives if they are in despair. Even Augustine cannot know himself fully, and he cannot know God fully. He inquires how he can know God. The physical world testifies to its creator, but the physical world is not God. Even animals have senses to perceive the world, but they cannot apply reason to lead them beyond physical things. The human soul orders the perceptions of the senses, but Augustine must ascend beyond this function, to memory.

Memory stores not only sense perceptions but also skills and ideas, which are not apprehended through the senses. Learning is the process of gathering and ordering all these notions in the memory. Mathematics is purely abstract, incapable of making sense impressions, but the memory can hold it. Emotions, too, can remain in the memory, although they have no existence outside the mind. People only remember those emotions, rather than feel them anew. The images of all these things are present in memory, but what about the idea of memory itself, or the idea of forgetfulness? How can I remember "forgetfulness" if forgetfulness is the very act of not remembering?

The power of human memory is vast and awesome, but how can one move beyond memory to knowledge of God? If you forget something, you can look for its image in your memory, if only partially. All people want to be happy, but how do people know of happiness? True happiness is only with God. Human beings mistake earthly happiness for the happiness found in God; people hide from this truth and so become miserable. God is not a sense perception, an emotion, or even the mind itself, but God remains in the memory.

Commentary

Book 10 is a distinct departure from the first nine books of the *Confessions*. Only now, after the story of his conversion is finished, does Augustine address the question of why he is writing. This question leads Augustine into a far-ranging discussion of the nature of the human mind, memory, and sense perceptions.

The simple answer to Augustine's question of "why write this story?" (and its corollary, "why read it?") is disposed of early on: Augustine's story can be an example to his fellow Christians, the people he has devoted his life to serving. Seeing Augustine, the good can be moved to praise God and give thanks for God's mercy; those stuck in the grasp of their sins can take hope and find energy to put those sins behind them. Augustine even asks the question his readers inevitably ask: How can they know that anything Augustine says is actually true? Augustine candidly admits that even he cannot really know everything about himself; only God has such perfect knowledge. Augustine does not try to avoid this fact or explain it away. His only reply is that love, the virtue that "believes all things," will lead his readers to discern the truth of what he says.

The more complex answer to Augustine's question is implied behind his long argument about the human mind and perception. The assumption, which Augustine never directly states, is that by knowing the self, human beings can begin to understand God. This is an idea borrowed from Platonism: Because the human spirit shares in some of the divinity of God, from which that spirit comes, knowledge of the inner self is also is some measure knowledge of the divine. This is not self-knowledge in the sense of contemplating one's own belly-button. Egotism and self-absorption are directly contrary to real knowledge of the self. The kind of self-knowledge Augustine wants is an understanding of the inner workings of the human soul, because those actions are initiated and should return to the divine. Augustine signals the nature of his quest by beginning it, in 4.7, with another reference to the Platonic ascent from the physical world to through the soul to the immaterial realm, as he presented in 7.17.

He proceeds through his argument in careful stages, asking how human beings acquire knowledge. The simplest kind of knowledge is received from the physical world. The human memory stores impressions received from the senses and allows them to be organized and recalled. But the mind also stores other kinds of "images" that are not physical: purely abstract concepts like mathematics, or human emotions, which do not exist outside the individual human mind. Likewise, Augustine concludes, the human memory stores an impression of the true happiness that is found only in God. Exactly how this is possible he does not say, but he implies that the memory retains a kind of memory of its existence in the divine realm or the substance that it shares with God. This memory of happiness accounts for the fact that all human beings, regardless of their personal differences, want to be happy. Inwardly, dimly, they long to regain this perfect happiness that they can now grasp only imperfectly because of their limited physical existence. The error that human beings commit is to substitute the limited happiness and pleasure that the physical realm gives for the ultimate happiness found in God. Human sinfulness means that human beings find it hateful to see this truth revealed to them. Sluggish and earthbound, the human mind languishes in a kind of inertia that keeps it from rising toward the true reality, foolishly confident in its own knowledge. Augustine himself is testimony to the fact that human beings can break free from this inertia—but only if they are aided by God's grace and accept God's will.

Augustine's dense discussion of human memory also demonstrates how deeply he values rationality. Augustine reasons his way toward these conclusions; they are not beyond human grasp, nor do they require secret knowledge or privileged revelations, such as the Manichees claimed to offer. The entire physical world offers evidence of these truths, if only the human eye looks carefully enough to see them.

Theme

Augustine's interest in language also appears throughout this section. The signs and symbols of language become associated with images in the memory, so that the sound of word recalls from the memory the image or idea it represents. These signs are not absolute. They vary among speakers of Latin and Greek, for example. Augustine's appreciation of language as a set of humanly constructed conventions has an unusually modern flavor and has attracted the attention of many post-modern analysts of language and literature. He further explores this subject, as well as extending his analysis of the human mind, in his treatise *De trinitate* (On the Trinity), begun at about the same time Augustine was writing the *Confessions*.

Book 10, Chapters 26–34

Summary

Wrongly in love with the beauty of the world, Augustine learned to love the beauty of God late in life. Whether one is rich or poor, life brings numerous temptations, from which only God can save people. Augustine considers the three kinds of temptations: lust of the senses, curiosity, and power. God gave Augustine strength to give up sexual activity, but his old habit still haunts him as erotic dreams. The pleasures of taste cannot so easily be given up, because one must eat. But one must be careful not to take inordinate pleasure in satisfying this need. The temptations of sweet smells are not difficult for Augustine to resist, but the temptations of sound, and especially music, are strong. When Augustine hears hymns sung, his reason takes pleasure in the words, but he is always tempted to let his irrational pleasure in the sounds themselves take over. The temptations of sight are impossible to avoid, because they are everywhere, in colors and light. Love of physical light can be sinful, but God himself offers spiritual light. All beautiful human arts and crafts come from God, but human beings do not move from these lower beauties to the higher beauty. Lust of the eyes is related to the second temptation, curiosity. Curiosity is a kind of craving after knowledge and experience for its own sake. Theater appeals to this craving, as does science, magic, and the demands of the faithful for signs and miracles. The third temptation is power. Human beings long to be feared or loved by others. Augustine admits he cannot control this temptation, because he can never disentangle his love for his fellow human beings from his own desire for approval.

Augustine meditates on his physical senses and his memory, and through them, he can sometimes ascend to a moment of contact with God, but he can never sustain it, so he falls back to his old self. Only Christ, who was fully human and fully God, can mediate between humans and God. Only Christ can cure Augustine's sins and give him hope.

Commentary

Theme

From memory and the knowledge of God, Augustine turns to the temptations of the world. He revisits the threefold causes of sin he first mentioned in Book 3.8 and that he derives from I John 2:16. "Lust of the senses" includes sexual lust, as it always has for Augustine, but here, Augustine examines in detail the temptations of all five senses. As Augustine remarks in the first half of Book 10, it is through the senses that humans receive knowledge of the world and begin to form the images of memory. The physical world and the bodily senses that perceive it are at the bottom of the Platonic ascent that leads the soul to God. Another point of this examination is that Augustine's spiritual journey did not end at his conversion or his baptism or at Ostia, where his narrative ended. He continues to struggle against temptation and to rely on God to bear him up. In fact, Augustine caps his discussion of each temptation with an appeal to God's grace and mercy to provide him the way to overcome that temptation. At the end of this literary examination of sin, Augustine describes himself meditatively examining his physical body—the report of his senses, the workings of his mind—until he makes the Platonic ascent and briefly achieves something like the beatific vision. The last part of Book 10, then, is a kind of literary acting out of the beginning stages of the ascent, in which Augustine and the reader jointly participate. But as in Book 7 and Book 10, the beatific vision cannot be sustained for long, because material human beings are too weak and limited to attain the immaterial realm. Only Christ, who was fully human as well as fully divine, can mediate between heaven and earth, spiritual and physical, God and humanity. Christ alone saves Augustine, and all humanity, from the abundant and unavoidable temptations and sins that plague them.

Modern readers are likely to be stupefied by Augustine's excruciatingly detailed examination of the dangers inherent in each of the senses. However, for Augustine, the dangers they represent are real. The temptation posed by all the senses, by curiosity, and by love of power is ultimately toward concupiscence, the immoderate love of the lower, physical goods that substitutes for healthy love of the highest good, God.

It is particularly hard for modern readers to view curiosity as a sin. The range of experiences that involve curiosity for Augustine is particularly eclectic: theater, the sciences, astrology, even the distractions of natural scenes. Curiosity for Augustine can include what may be thought of as morbid curiosity. It can also include intellectual pride; Augustine does not condemn all observation of the natural, but he does condemn seeking knowledge of the created world for its own sake and for the achievement of having understood it, rather than for what it can reveal about its creator. Curiosity can mean sticking one's nose into areas it does not belong, as in trying to predict the future or unveil the mysteries of universe. The *curiositas* of theater is a kind of sensationalism, an itching for cheap thrills. Even devout Christians can be guilty of being curious when they crave miracles and signs from God, in a kind of spiritual thrill-seeking. All of these curiosities distract the mind from seeking for substance in God.

Character Insight

Augustine displays acute knowledge of his own failings here, and nowhere is he more honest than in his examination of his own pride. Augustine loves to be loved; he enjoys doing well and being praised for it. These facets of his character are evident even in his description of himself as a child. But sin is so entangled with human behavior that Augustine cannot pull out one pure motive for his acceptance of praise. If someone praises his statements, is he pleased because of his neighbor's spiritual progress, or is he pleased because his vanity is flattered? For Augustine, this knot cannot be untied; only Christ can absolve humankind of its painful contradictions.

Glossary

Athanasius   c. 296–373, bishop of Alexandria, theologian, and saint, noted for his asceticism.

Book 11, Chapters 1–31

Summary

Augustine considers the meaning of the first words of Genesis: "In the beginning, God created heaven and earth." Augustine asks how he can know that this is true. It is obvious that all things were created, because they are subject to change. God created them through the Word, Jesus Christ. The Word is co-eternal with God and not created. People ask what God was doing in the time before he created the world. Augustine replies that there was no time, because God created time itself. Augustine considers the nature of time. One can speak of past, present, and future time, but the past has ceased to be, the future is not yet, and only the present exists, but the present moment cannot have any duration. But if this is true, how can one speak of history, or how can prophets foresee future events? The human memory retains images of past events. Perhaps some can predict the future by reading likely signs of what will happen. How do people measure time? The movement of the sun and planets is not time, as many assert. Augustine concludes that time is a "distension" of the mind; what human beings measure is the impression that things or events make on them. Augustine is torn and divided by time, but God alone is eternal and unchanging.

Commentary

Theme

Having addressed the subject of memory in Book 10, Augustine now moves on to the nature of time itself. God's creation of the world, as described in Genesis, forms the basis of the final three books of the *Confessions,* and many readers have had difficulty seeing the connection between these three books and the first ten. However, a consideration of time is not completely out of place in a work that relies so much upon the memory of past events. Augustine himself frames his discussion of time by referring to his own act of writing the *Confessions.* He is confessing the times of his own life, the past events that live in his memory, so he asks, what is the nature of time?

As always, Augustine lays out his argument in careful stages. First, he considers God, the creator of all things and of time itself. As Augustine noted in other sections of the *Confessions,* God is timeless. God dwells in eternity, outside human notions of past, present, or future. Therefore, it is irrelevant to ask how God occupied his time before he created the world, because there was no such thing as time. As part of this argument, Augustine engages in another bit of Christology, as he did near the end of Book 7. Genesis says that God created the world by speaking, and that speech was the Word, or the *Logos,* as described at the beginning of the Gospel of John, which Augustine has already quoted at length at 7.9. As the Word, Christ is not a created thing, but is co-eternal with God.

So if time is not divine and transcendent, what is it? Augustine embarks on an analysis of time that quickly becomes absurd: The distinguishing characteristic of time is that it tends toward non-existence! If neither the past nor the future exist, then only an infinitesimally small moment of the present can be said to actually exist. But Augustine recognizes the absurdity of the argument and pulls back from it. Everyday language about time may be inaccurate, he concedes, but still, people manage to understand each other. He considers a second argument, that time is the movement of the heavenly bodies such as the sun and stars. This, too, is incorrect, Augustine concludes. These things are simply indicators that humankind uses to mark the passing of time, and in this sense, the revolutions of the planets are no different than the spinning of a potter's wheel as devices for marking regular intervals of time.

Finally, Augustine gets to the crux of his argument: If time does not exist, how can people talk about the past or the future, or a "long time" or "short time," as all human beings do? Time is really a function of human memory and perception, Augustine decides. Augustine uses a unique Latin term for this function: *distentio,* usually translated as an "extension" or "distension" of the mind. These terms reflect a sense of tension, or even of painful stretching, that the perception of time creates. Three functions of the mind relate to this distension: attention, which focuses on the present; memory, which focuses on the past; and expectation, which focuses on the future. Interestingly, Augustine draws all his examples for these functions from human language: He compares syllables and lines of poetry to demonstrate how people perceive sound events and rhythms as longer or shorter, and the act of reciting a memorized psalm as an example of memory, attention, and expectation. Only at the end of 11.28 does Augustine move this argument out into the realm of broader human experience, as he observes that what is true of the psalm is true of the events of human life (like Augustine's own life story in the *Confessions*) and the whole of human history.

Time, for Augustine, is a painful affair, a reflection of the limited material nature of human beings. The perception of time leaves human beings torn, fragmented, confused by jumbled events. Only God, living in eternity, is free from the confusions of time. Significantly, words are always stuck in time: sounding, then falling silent, following one another sequentially to create meaning. Augustine's narrative, made as it must be of time-bound words, is similarly stuck in time, unable to rise above the inherent limitations of language. As in Book 10, questions of language become related to questions of credibility. Augustine asks, how can he know that Moses (the traditional author of Genesis) was telling the truth? How can anyone know what he meant? If he could question Moses, would Augustine even understand the answer, given that Augustine himself does not speak Hebrew, and Moses would not speak Latin? Language and time are both veils that cover human understanding, obscuring the perfect vision of divine eternity, where there are no sequences, no divisions, no passing into nonexistence, no past or future. All human language is only a pale shadow of the eternal Word, and yet language is humanity's vehicle for thinking about God and communicating God's revelation throughout human history. Only in the beatific vision, the direct contact with God that human beings cannot sustain, does one find a taste of what God's timelessness is like.

Book 12, Chapters 1–31

Summary

Augustine examines the second verse of Genesis: "The earth was invisible and formless, darkness was over the deep." He says that "heaven" does not mean the sky, but the immaterial "heaven of heavens," and "earth" does not mean the ground, but the formless matter that is the basis of all physical forms. Augustine imagines opponents who disagree with his interpretation. They say that Moses intended "heaven and earth" to mean the visible world only. Augustine proposes other possible interpretations. He concludes that multiple true interpretations of the passage exist and do not contradict each other. Augustine and his opponents can say with confidence that the message Moses conveyed is true, but they cannot be so confident that they know precisely what Moses intended his words to mean. Surely Moses would have tried to make his words convey as much depth of meaning as possible.

Commentary

Book 12 finds Augustine engaged even more deeply in the practice of exegesis that he began in Book 11. Exegesis is the act of interpreting a Biblical text, and few Christian thinkers have raised it to such an art form as Augustine. In Book 12, you can see some of Augustine's principles of exegesis in action, although he lays out his theories more explicitly in *On Christian Doctrine,* which he was writing at about the same time as the *Confessions.* Most notably, Augustine's interpretation of Genesis 1:2 moves immediately beyond the literal sense of the words to a spiritual, almost metaphorical sense. Augustine's understanding of the Creation is heavily influenced by the ideas of Platonism, as his descriptions of the realms of immaterial intellect and formless matter reflect. Heaven, for Augustine, is instantly identifiable as the "heaven of heavens" of Psalm 155:16: "The heaven of heaven is the Lord's: but the earth he has given to the children of men." This "heaven of heavens" has multiple properties: It is immaterial and it is outside time, although it is not co-eternal with God and is not made of God's own substance—only the Word, the first Wisdom, Jesus Christ, has that distinction. But the "heaven of heavens" is also identified with God's wisdom; see Ecclesiasticus 1:3–4: "Who has searched out the wisdom of God that goes before all things? Wisdom has been created before all things, and the understanding of prudence from everlasting." Furthermore, Augustine also identifies the "heaven of heavens" with the immaterial realm of the intellect, where knowledge is received directly, without mediation, and simultaneously, without the passage of time. This may refer both to God's intellect and to the human intellect, created in the image of the divine. In this way, the "heaven of heavens" sounds very much like the beatific vision of Books 7 and 10, which human minds can attain, but not for long.

Heaven's opposite number is earth; not the literal ground underfoot, but the formless matter from which God later created all physical forms. The existence of such undifferentiated matter is a tenet of Platonism, here placed into a Christian framework. Augustine has almost as much difficulty trying to visualize truly formless matter as he previously did trying to visualize a truly immaterial God. Formless matter was created from nothing and is only a little above nothingness, but from it, God created the physical world, including what people normally think of as heaven and earth. That process of differentiation and assigning forms is described in Genesis' account of the different "days" of creation.

Augustine's method of exegesis is rich and multi-layered. Every Biblical text is influenced by a web of other scriptural texts that touch on it and expand its meaning, as Psalm 116 does for Genesis 1:2. The meaning of a particular word may include its literal sense, but it also includes spiritual, metaphorical, and symbolic meanings as well. Here, you see demonstrated the qualities that so perplexed Augustine when he attempted to study the Bible in Books 3.5 and 9.5: The words of the Bible appear simple enough, but for those attentive students who examine them closely, they unfold complex and multivalent possibilities.

Theme

While Augustine shows the greatest respect for his text, giving each word the most detailed consideration, and while he believes without question that the text is divinely inspired, he does acknowledge an important limitation: Words are only words. Readers cannot question Moses about exactly what he intended when he wrote those words. One can only look at the words, and words are necessarily limited, imprecise, subject to interpretation. Augustine decides to err on the side of charity: If a passage supports multiple interpretations, then why not allow all of them to be true? Only human vanity insists that one's own interpretation is the sole correct interpretation. Contemporary scholars of literature and language have been intrigued by Augustine's very modern concern with the shortcomings of language, the unknowable intent of the author and the multiplicity of meanings. However, Augustine would never support the modern assertion that all possible interpretations are equally valid or that the meaning of a text can never be located with certainty. Interpretations that offend basic Christian doctrine cannot be true, and logic can be applied as a test, as well—we see Augustine logically analyzing different possible interpretations in 12.28–29. Incidentally, the opponents Augustine invents to argue with him about exegesis do not seem to refer to any specific group. They may simply function in the text as a sounding board for Augustine's ideas. The dialogue form was a common classical device for writing about philosophical ideas.

How, then, does this Neo-Platonic exegetical exercise function within the structure of the *Confessions?* As with Augustine's interpretations, several possibilities exist. If one of the subjects of the *Confessions* is Augustine's attempt to understand God and his own relationship to God, then exegesis of Genesis does further that goal. The story of the Creation defines what the divine and the human are, and the subsequent story of the Fall defines how their relationship to one another went wrong. This extended attempt at interpretation also demonstrates that Augustine's spiritual journey is far from over, as Augustine must continue to expand and deepen his understanding of God. Throughout his career as a bishop, Augustine is pressed explain the mysteries of scripture in the sermons he gives to his congregation, and many of his major works consist of in-depth examinations of Biblical passages, so Book 12 may serve a teaching function, as well. Finally, Augustine uses the opportunity to explain, and, therefore, to defend, his Neo-Platonic influences by showing how seamlessly they fit with Christian beliefs.

Book 13, Chapters 1–38

Summary

All of creation depends on God's goodness, and God chose to create because of the abundance of his goodness. Augustine examines the action of the Holy Trinity in the creation by looking at the verse "the Spirit moved over the waters." Just as a human has being, knowledge, and will but is one person, so the Holy Trinity has those qualities but is one God. Augustine examines the rest of the Genesis creation story: He interprets "the firmament" as the holy scriptures, "the sea and the dry land" as the unfaithful and the Church, "bearing fruit" as the good works of the faithful, "moving things of the sea and winged things that fly" as the sacraments and miracles, "let us make man in our image" as rebirth through belief in Christ, "beasts" as the impulses of the soul, "increase and multiply" as referring to the thoughts of human reason, "food" as the joy found in knowledge of God. The Holy Spirit allows people to see and know these truths. The last day of the creation was for rest; so, too, will the faithful rest with God on the eternal Sabbath day.

Commentary

Theme

Book 13 opens with a restatement of Augustine's theme from the opening of Book 1: the utter dependence of human beings upon God, even for the impulses of faith and for the desire to return to God. Augustine recalls his wanderings and his return to rest in the God who constantly called him back. Even light itself, the spiritual light meant by God's creating command, "let there be light," seeks to return and gaze upon God. In Book 13, Augustine makes clear the identification between himself, humanity, and the entire creation. All three have fallen away from God, all three long to return, and all three depend completely upon God for the ability to love God and to turn themselves toward God. In this way, Augustine's story is not only his own; it is a metaphor for human fallenness, and for the longing of the entire created universe to rest at last in its perfect and eternal Creator.

As you may expect from the highly figurative interpretations of Genesis 1:1–2 in Books 11 and 12, Augustine finds in the creation story a metaphor for the creation and life of the Church, the community of the Christian faithful, which is sustained by the action of the Holy Spirit, the third aspect of the Holy Trinity. Although Augustine initially mentions the Trinity in Book 12.7, here, the Trinity gets much fuller treatment, as Augustine explains the properties of the three "persons" of the One God. The Father can be identified with being or existence: God the Father is eternal, perfect, and unchanging. The Son can be identified with knowledge: God the Son is the Word, the eternal Wisdom that gave order and meaning to the creation. The Holy Spirit can be identified with the will: God the Holy Spirit is the activity of God, at work throughout history and specifically within the body of the Church. Augustine identifies these qualities of the Trinity with qualities of human beings, reinforcing Augustine's notion that humanity is created in the spiritual image of God. J.J. O'Donnell and other scholars have noted that the Trinity also serves as a structural element for the last three books of the *Confessions:* Book 11, with its contrasts between human time and God's eternity, corresponds to the "being" of God; Book 12, with its intense focus on the textual word of God as contrasted to the eternal Word who is Christ, corresponds to the "knowledge" of God; and Book 13, with its focus on the activity and faith journey the Church as sustained by the Holy Spirit, corresponds to the "will" of God.

In Augustine's hands, the rest of the creation story becomes a miniature history of the Church: "Dry land" becomes the community of the faithful, thirsty for God, while the "seas" of the world of unbelievers rage restlessly around them. The crux of this history comes in God's statement "let us make man in our image." For Augustine, God's statement of creation is literally a command to spiritual rebirth. To become a person made in "God's image" means to accept Christ fully—to "put on Christ," as Augustine read under the pear tree, and thereby become a new person, leaving behind the old Adam. This has been Augustine's journey, but it is also the journey that every member of the Church—and in Augustine's view, every human being—is called to make.

Book 1 of the *Confessions* opens with the observation that "our heart is restless until it rests in you." It is, therefore, appropriate that Augustine ends Book 13 with rest. Literally, it is the rest of the Sabbath day, the seventh day of the Genesis story, when God rested from the work of creation (Genesis 2:1). Figuratively, it is the rest of eternal life, and more importantly, the rest that the soul finds upon its return to God. Augustine introduces a particularly interesting figure in Book 13.9, where he observes that love is the weight that pulls him into his proper place. The Platonic ascent of the soul is one of Augustine's major themes throughout the *Confessions:* Poised between the immaterial realm of God and the material realm of the physical world, the human soul attempts to rise toward God, leaving behind lesser, material things. Normally, the "weight" that pulls Augustine down, away from God, is his physical being, the temptations of the material world—specifically, for Augustine, the "weight" of sexual desire. But in 13.9, love is the weight that pulls Augustine not downward, but toward his proper place. Augustine's metaphor here is flame, whose "weight" draws it upward. Not coincidentally, flame is also the symbolic attribute of the Holy Spirit (see Acts 2:3), the subject of Book 13. The love that the Holy Spirit brings is exactly the opposite of cupidity, and it is this love that draws Augustine into his own proper equilibrium.

Glossary

the fish   a symbol for Christ, from the phrase "Jesus Christ, God's Son, Savior," whose first letters in Greek spell the Greek word for "fish."

Galatians   quoting from Paul's letter rebuking the Christians in Galatia for insisting on the observance of Jewish law, rather than relying upon faith (Gal. 3:1).

friend of the bridegroom   a reference to John 3:29: "The friend who attends the bridegroom waits and listens for him and is full of joy when he hears the bridegroom's voice." In its original context, the "friend" is John the Baptist, but Augustine is applying the symbolism more broadly, to any faithful soul.

Onesiphorus   praised for his assistance to St. Paul in 2 Timothy 1:16.

Epaphroditus   a companion of St. Paul; see Philippians 2:25–30. Paul thanks the Christian community at Philippi for their gifts to him, sent via Epahproditus (Philippians 4:18).

Elijah (or Elias)   prophet of the Old Testament. He is miraculously fed by a poor widow (1 Kings 17:9–24) and by ravens (1 Kings 17:6).

CRITICAL ESSAYS

The Confessions and Autobiography ... 81

Augustine's View of Sexuality 82

The *Confessions* and Autobiography

At its most basic, an autobiography is the story of a person's life, written by that person. It is sometimes said that Augustine invented the modern autobiography. Augustine did not simply establish a pattern; he produced a work whose influence was so pervasive that all later autobiographers were affected by it, either positively or negatively. (The most famous example of a reaction against Augustine's *Confessions* appears in the *Confessions* of Jean-Jacques Rousseau, the French Romantic writer and philosopher.) However, Augustine's *Confessions* was certainly not the first work of autobiography in Western literature. Numerous Classical authors had produced stories of their own lives, and Augustine also had specifically Christian examples to draw on, such as the passion narratives of martyred saints like Perpetua.

However, Augustine's autobiography is unique in several ways. The *Confessions* is not a straightforward account of the events of Augustine's life. In fact, Augustine frequently leaves out events that readers may consider important. The death of his father, for example, is mentioned only in passing, and large portions of his life are simply glossed over. On the other hand, Augustine gives special emphasis to seemingly small events, such as the theft of pears. In telling the story of his life, Augustine selects only those events that illustrate his spiritual development; everything else is pushed into the background. In focusing so tightly on his spiritual life, Augustine also trains his acute powers of observation on his own psychology. The intensely personal nature of Augustine's self-portrait is one of the aspects that has made it so appealing over the centuries. In the *Confessions,* Augustine is a fully rounded person: candid, acerbic, passionate, ambitious, restlessly intellectual, devoted to his friends, subject to flaws of pride and excess. Augustine's voice is uniquely identifiable, and it gives readers a genuine feel for his personality and character. Readers see Augustine not only from the outside, but from the inside.

By its nature, autobiography is a tricky genre. Because autobiography has an element of history, readers expect some measure of historical accuracy from the author. But because autobiography is also a form of literature, it shares some of the elements of fiction: a story arc, specific events that move the story, and details of style and narrative that affect your interpretation. Readers, therefore, may wonder how much of an autobiography is true. This question does not necessarily imply deliberate deception on the part of the author; human memory is naturally selective, and your perceptions of your own life are shaped by your experiences. Throughout the *Confessions,* readers are constantly confronted with two Augustines: the young Augustine struggling along his spiritual path, and the older Augustine, the narrator, who looks back over this path and finds that it had a direction he was unable to recognize at the time.

By being selective about the events he chooses in order to illustrate his life, Augustine is giving a deliberate shape to his narrative, a shape that the messy events of life generally do not possess. As an author, he is aware of the tricks that memory can play; he devotes much attention to examining how memory works. Furthermore, Augustine gives his story a distinct arc, as event builds upon event in Augustine's spiritual struggle. Augustine also uses clear literary echoes to lend meaning to his story. He repeatedly compares himself to the Prodigal Son, the wandering sinner returning home, and when he abandons Monica at Carthage, his story parallels that of another famous wanderer, Aeneas. The scholar Pierre Courcelle, examining the *Confessions,* identified literary parallels for almost every part of Augustine's story. But does that mean the story is fictional?

In one sense, to ask whether the *Confessions* is empirically true is to ask the wrong question. You have only the story as Augustine tells it, and ultimately, you must judge it on its own merits. The game of "hunt the author" can quickly become an exercise in absurdity. Scholars have spent considerable time and energy, for example, debating what exactly happened to Augustine in his garden at Milan: What could a child from that period of history have said, in the course of a game or a conversation, that Augustine would have misheard or interpreted as "Take and read"? Such questions may be entertaining, but they do not shed much light on the meaning of the *Confessions,* either for Augustine as writer or for his readers. As Augustine's own interpretations of Christian scripture demonstrate, he was always looking for the meanings hidden under the surface of a text, and he believed that even seemingly simple texts could support multiple interpretations. For Augustine, historical truth and symbolic significance were not mutually exclusive. If you view the *Confessions* as both autobiography and literary artwork, you can open up your understanding of it in ways that the *Confessions* itself invites.

Augustine's View of Sexuality

One of the most notable features of the *Confessions,* and one that has fascinated—or perhaps titillated—readers through the centuries is

Augustine's honesty about his sexual career. Augustine makes clear that he was no angel: As a young man, he was sexually active, and later, he lived openly with a concubine who bore him a son. As Augustine describes himself, he was a slave to his sexual impulses. Reader response to this candor has varied over the centuries. Many critics have taken Augustine at his word that he was a libertine. However, most modern scholars have questioned just how well Augustine's view of himself would have squared with the views his contemporaries. In living with a concubine, he was not necessarily much different from other men of his time, and it is certainly possible that his descriptions of his sexual exploits are exaggerated. Augustine's sexual impulses were clearly a source of intense emotional pain for him, and this fact alone may account for the emphasis he places on his sexual sins.

Throughout the *Confessions,* the language Augustine uses to describe his sexual impulses is negative, reflecting images of disease, disorder, and corruption. Desire is mud (2.2, 3.1), a whirlpool (2.2), chains (2.2, 3.1) thorns (2.3), a seething cauldron (3.1), and an open sore that must be scratched (3.1). Desire for Augustine is almost a compulsion, an irrational impulse that he feels incapable of controlling without God's help, a bondage that he is too weak to escape. Desire becomes the last obstacle between Augustine and a complete commitment to God, because he is certain he cannot live a celibate life.

Augustine was not unique in his negative attitudes toward sexuality. During this period, extreme asceticism was a standard to be admired and emulated. The heroes of Augustine's Christian contemporaries were spiritual athletes like St. Antony, who gave up even the most innocent pleasures to live as a hermit in the desert. During Augustine's lifetime, there were numerous examples of old-line Roman aristocrats who, upon conversion, gave away their wealth to the poor and the Church, lived voluntarily in celibate marriages, and withdrew from Roman society to dedicate their entire lives to the contemplation of God. In the story that Ponticianus tells Augustine, not only the two young Roman officials but also their fiancées instantly decide to give up everything—including sex and marriage—to dedicate themselves fully to God. Against such a backdrop, Augustine's assertion that there may be a legitimate outlet for sexuality, in marriage and the procreation of children, sounds almost radically liberal.

Nonetheless, it is Augustine's negative views about sexuality that predominate. In her book *Adam, Eve, and the Serpent,* the religious scholar Elaine Pagels is critical of Augustine's equation of sex with original sin, identifying Augustine as a source of Western society's negative attitudes about sexuality. Whether Augustine is directly responsible for the traditions that came down to history or simply articulated the prevailing viewpoint is open to debate. However, Augustine clearly had a significant influence in shaping Western ideas about sexuality.

CliffsNotes Review

Use this CliffsNotes Review to test your understanding of the original text, and reinforce what you've learned in this book. After you work through the review and essay questions, identify the quote section, and the fun and useful practice projects, you're well on your way to understanding a comprehensive and meaningful interpretation of St. Augustine and *Confessions.*

Q & A

1. To what religion did Augustine belong before converting to Catholic Christianity?

_____

2. At what city did Augustine and his mother Monica experience a vision of heaven?

_____

3. What vision does Monica see that reassures her Augustine will return to Christianity?

_____

4. What does Augustine identify as the three types of sin?

_____

Answers: (1) Manichaeism. (2) The port city of Ostia, where Monica died and was buried. (3) She sees herself standing upon a ruling stick, and a young man tells her that where she is, Augustine will be. She then sees Augustine standing with her on the ruler. (4) Lust of the eyes *(curiositas),* lust of the senses *(concupiscence),* and lust for domination (pride).

Identify the Quote

1. Our heart is restless until it rests in you.

_____

2. Grant what you command and command what you will.

_____

3. Give me chastity, but not yet.

_____

4. It cannot be that the son of these tears should perish.

_____

5. Take and read.

_____

Answers: (1) From Book 1.1; this statement reflects on Augustine's spiritual wanderings and his role as the Prodigal Son who at last returns home to God. (2) From Book 10.9; this statement shows Augustine's insistence on the absolute dependence of human beings on God's grace. (3) From Book 8.7; this statement reflects Augustine's obsession with sexual desire and his feeling at the time that it would be impossible to live a celibate life. (4) From Book 3.12; this is the statement of the ex-Manichee bishop whom Monica visits, to ask him to speak to convince Augustine of the errors of Manichaeism. (5) From Book 8.12; these are the words of the mysterious child's voice Augustine hears in his garden. He interprets this voice as a command to pick up his book of St. Paul's Epistles.

Essay Questions

1. Discuss Augustine's concept of *curiositas*. What qualities distinguish *curiositas*, and what actions does it include? Why does Augustine view it as a source of sin?

2. Analyze the character of Monica. Describe her relationship with Augustine and her role within the *Confessions*. What are her distinguishing characteristics? To what extent is she a stereotypical mother figure, or does she have realistic qualities?

3. Discuss Augustine's attitudes toward friendship. What are the qualities of true friendship? How do friends influence one another? Does friendship have any negative qualities?

4. Consider Augustine's definition of time as a "distension." What does he mean by this word? How does the human perception of time compare to God's perception of time?

5. Language is an important topic in the *Confessions*. What issues revolve around the use and abuse of language for Augustine? What are the values and shortcomings of language? How do these issues impact Augustine as an author?

6. Examine Augustine's statements about free will in the *Confessions*. To what degree are human beings really free to make their own choices? How is the problem of evil connected with the human will? Do you agree with Augustine's conclusions?

7. Create a chart or diagram illustrating the plot structure of the *Confessions,* and then discuss the structure you see. Based on your analysis, do the 13 books of the *Confessions* form a unified whole or not?

8. Describe Augustine's attitude toward the material world. Does he portray it as good or bad? What appeals or temptations does it hold? How might Augustine's attitudes have been influenced by the Manichees or the Neo-Platonists?

9. Examine Augustine's comments about women and women's roles in the *Confessions*. Where do women appear (and not appear) in the text? What does Augustine see as the proper relationship between men and women? How might his view of sexuality influence his ideas about women?

10. Describe Augustine's relationship to his God. How does he envision God at the different stages of his spiritual journey? What qualities does Augustine ascribe to God?

Practice Projects

1. Compare and contrast the *Confessions* with another work of autobiography. (Suggestions include Jean-Jacques Rousseau's *Confessions,* Gertrude Stein's *Autobiography of Alice B. Toklas,* or the *Autobiography of Malcolm X,* by Malcolm X with Alex Haley.) What are the authors' goals in telling their life stories? What strategies do they use to give shape to the events of their lives?

2. Augustine presents a distinctly Christian story in the *Confessions*. Critique Augustine's assumptions about the relationship between God and humanity from the point of view of another world religion, such as Islam or Buddhism, or from an atheist viewpoint.

CliffsNotes Resource Center

The learning doesn't need to stop here. CliffsNotes Resource Center shows you the best of the best—links to the best information in print and online about the author and/or related works. And don't think that this is all we've prepared for you; we've put all kinds of pertinent information at www.cliffsnotes.com. Look for all the terrific resources at your favorite bookstore or local library and on the Internet. When you're online, make your first stop www.cliffsnotes.com where you'll find more incredibly useful information about St. Augustine and *Confessions*.

Books and Articles

This CliffsNotes book provides a meaningful interpretation of *Confessions*. If you are looking for information about the author and/or related works, check out these other publications. **Translations:**

Dozens of English-language translations of the Confessions are available to students, but three deserve special mention: F.J. Sheed's 1942 translation has been praised for capturing some of the rhetorical elegance of Augustine's Latin. R.S. Pine-Coffin's 1962 translation is more easily readable for beginners. Henry Chadwick's 1991 translation is also accessible and offers many helpful footnotes.

The standard Latin edition of the *Confessions* is is a three-volume set edited by James J. O'Donnell (Oxford University Press, 1992). While only scholars of Latin will benefit from the text itself, O'Donnell's excellent introductory essays and extensive commentary are in English.

BROWN, PETER S. *Augustine of Hippo.* Berkeley: University of California Press, 2000. (New edition, with an epilogue.) The standard scholarly biography of Augustine.

CLARK, GILLIAN. *Augustine: The Confessions.* Cambridge: Cambridge University Press, 1993. (Landmarks of World Literature Series). One of the few books on the *Confessions* designed for students unfamiliar with Augustine.

FITZGERALD, ALLAN D., ed. *Augustine through the Ages: An Encyclopedia.* Grand Rapid, MI: Eerdmans, 1999. A helpful reference book for students of Augustine and the *Confessions,* featuring numerous well-written articles on all things Augustine.

O'CONNELL, ROBERT J. *St. Augustine's Confessions.* Cambridge, MA: Harvard University Press, 1969. A helpful analysis that examines the *Confessions* book by book.

O'DONNELL, JAMES J. *Augustine.* Boston: Twayne, 1985. (Twayne's World Authors Series.). A brief intellectual biography of Augustine, focusing on the major themes in his thought.

O'MEARA, JOHN J. *The Young Augustine: An Introduction to the Confessions of St. Augustine.* London: Longman, 1954. Examines the *Confessions* with special attention to Augustine's life and early thought.

POWER, KIM. *Veiled Desire: Augustine on Women.* New York: Crossroad, 1992. Useful background about how women were viewed in Augustine's society, plus analyses of Augustine's relations with women as a son, a lover, and a cleric.

> It's easy to find books published by Wiley Publishing, Inc. You'll find them in your favorite bookstores (on the Internet and at a store near you). We also have three Web sites that you can use to read about all the books we publish:
>
> ■ www.cliffsnotes.com
>
> ■ www.dummies.com
>
> ■ www.wiley.com

Internet

Check out these Web resources for more information about St. Augustine and the *Confessions:*

Augustine of Hippo, http://ccat.sas.upenn.edu/jod/augustine.html—maintained by J.J. O'Donnell, one of the leading Augustine scholars and the author of the standard critical edition (in Latin) of the *Confessions.* The complete Latin text, with O'Donnell's English commentary, is available at this site, along with a wealth of other material related to Augustine.

Internet Medieval Sourcebook: The End of the Classical World, www.fordham.edu/halsall/sbook1b.html—helpful introduction to the history and culture of Augustine's age.

Saint Augustine: Stanford Encyclopedia of Philosophy, http://plato.stanford.edu/entries/augustine/—a brief but helpful introduction to Augustine's life and thought.

Index

A

Academics, 44
Adam, Eve, and the Serpent (Elaine Pagels), 83–84
Adeodatus (son), 2, 35, 50, 60, 61
adolescence, observations about, 25
Alypius (friend), 8, 46, 47–48, 58, 60
ambition
    spiritual, 56
    worldly, 26, 50–51
Ambrose (bishop), 3, 43, 45, 48, 61–62
Ambrosian chant, 61
Antony of the Desert (saint), 58, 83
Arianism, 62
Aristotle, *Categories*, 39, 40
asceticism, extreme, 83
astrology, 34–35, 52–53
astronomy, 41
Augustine (James O'Donnell), 89
Augustine of Hippo (Peter Brown), 88
Augustine of Hippo Web site, 89
Augustine (saint)
    beliefs of, 5
    birth of, 2
    career of, 3–4, 34
    City of God Against the Pagans, The, 4, 6
    De trinitate, 67
    death of, 6
    education of, 2–3, 29
    On Christian Doctrine, 38, 42, 74
    On the Beautiful and the Fitting, 39
    Retractiones, 6, 8
Augustine: The Confessions (Gillian Clark), 88
Augustine through the Ages: An Encyclopedia (Allan Fitzgerald), 88
autobiography, 59, 81–82

B

baptism, 20, 21, 37, 61
Bible, views of, 30
bishop, ex-Manichee, 33, 86
Brown, Peter, *Augustine of Hippo*, 88

C

Cassiciacum, 61
Categories (Aristotle), 39, 40
Catholics and Catholicism, 4, 44
celibacy, 26
Chadwick, Henry (translator), 88
childhood, observations about, 20, 23–24

Christian church, 4
Christology, 53–54, 72
Cicero, *Hortensius*, 2–3, 9, 29, 30
circus games, 47
City of God Against the Pagans, The (St. Augustine), 4, 6
Clark, Gillian, *Augustine: The Confessions*, 89
CliffsNotes Web site, 88, 89
concubine, relationship with, 35, 36, 50
concupiscence, 32, 69
confession
    meaning of, 8
    as praise, 17
Confessions (Jean-Jacques Rousseau), 81
Confessions (St. Augustine)
    motivation to write, 8, 48, 66
    structure of, 8–9, 76, 78
    synopsis of, 13–14
    translations of, 89
Continence, Lady, 59
conversion
    digression from story of, 59
    emotional, 53–54, 57–58
    "first," 30
    of friend, 37
    to Manichaeism, 31–32
    meaning of, 9
    as ongoing, 69
    public or external, 3, 55–56, 60
    story of, 17
creation story as metaphor, 77–78
curiositas, 32, 70
curiosity as sin, 69–70

D

De trinitate (St. Augustine), 67
death and change, 60–61
dependence upon God, 77
dialogue form, 76
disobedience, punishment for, 21
distentio, 72
Donatists, 4
dreams, 32

E

education, views of, 20–21, 23
Enneads (Plotinus), 10
eternity, 19
evil, problem of, 53
exegesis, 74–76

F

fame, observations on, 39–40
Faustus (bishop), 41, 42, 45
fig tree, 58–59
Fitzgerald, Allan, *Augustine through the Ages: An Encyclopedia*, 89

flame metaphor, 79
foreshadowing, 58
forgiveness and baptism, 21
friendship, nature of, 37, 38, 51

G

"Give me chastity, but not yet.", 86
Gnostic religions, 11
"Grant what you command and command
    what you will.", 86
grief, excessive, 37

H

habit, giving up bad, 46–47, 58, 63
happiness, 67
"heaven of heavens," 74–75
Holy Trinity, 78
Hortensius (Cicero), 2–3, 9, 29, 30
human sexuality, 5. *See also* sexual sin, attitude toward
human weakness, 16

I

infancy, observations about, 18, 19
intelligence, 40
Internet Medieval Sourcebook: The End of the Classical
    World Web site, 88
"It cannot be that the son of these tears should
    perish.", 86

J

Julian of Eclanum (advocate of Pelagianism), 5
Justina (mother of Valentinian), 61–62

K

knowledge, acquisition of, 66–67, 69, 75

L

language. *See also* style and language
    inadequacy of, 19
    interest in and appreciation for, 67
    as key to entry into human society, 20
    limitations of, 75–76
    understanding and, 73
literary device
    foreshadowing, 58
    metaphor, 55–56, 58–59, 77–78, 79
    personification, 59
love
    Holy Spirit and, 79
    selfish nature of, 44
    truth and, 66
    of wrongdoing, 27–28

M

Mani (prophet), 11
Manichaeism, 3, 11–13, 31–32, 41, 44
Manichee community, 44
Manichee Hearer, 34
Marcellinus (friend), 4
marriage
    as rescue from sin, 26
    wealth, ambition, and, 50
material world, view of, 18
memory
    acquisition of knowledge and, 66–67
    autobiography and, 81–82
    time and, 72
messages from God, 32, 33, 35, 37
metaphor, 55–56, 58–59, 77–78, 79
Milan, 45, 61
mind, functions of, 72
Monica (mother)
    arranged marriage and, 3, 50
    character of, 36
    on chastity, 26
    communication from God, 32, 33
    death of, 63, 64
    death of husband and, 30
    Manichaeism and, 31
    in Milan, 46–47
    move to Rome and, 43–44
    religion and, 2, 21, 22
    vision at Ostia, 64
moral perfection, 5
morality, exploration of, 31–32
music, 61

N

narrative, intimacy of, 17
Navigius (brother), 50
Nebridius (friend), 36, 46, 60, 61
Neo-Platonism, 10–11, 13, 39, 76. *See also* Platonism
North Africa, 2, 4, 5–6

O

O'Connell, Robert, *St. Augustine's Confessions*, 89
O'Donnell, James
    Augustine, 89
    essays and commentary of, 88
O'Meara, John, *The Young Augustine: An Introduction to
    the Confessions of St. Augustine*, 89
On Christian Doctrine (St. Augustine), 38, 42, 74
On the Beautiful and the Fitting (St. Augustine), 39
original sin, 5, 18–19, 29–30, 83–84
Ostia, 63
"Our heart is restless until it rests in you.", 86

P

pagan philosophy, 41, 42
Pagels, Elaine, *Adam, Eve, and the Serpent*, 83–84
parents, views on, 26. *See also* Monica; Patricius
Patricius (father), 2, 21–22, 26, 30
Paulinus of Nola (aristocrat), 8, 48
pears, theft of, 27–28
peer pressure, 28, 47
Pelagianism, 4, 5
Pelagius (monk), 4–5
personification, 59
physical, abandonment of for spiritual, 47
Pine-Coffin, R. S. (translator), 89
Plato (philosopher), 9
Platonic ascent of soul, 53, 69, 78–79
Platonism. *See also* Neo-Platonism
    exegesis and, 74, 75
    influence of, 9–10, 31
    self-knowledge and, 66
    as theoretical framework, 53
Plotinus (philosopher), 10
Ponticianus (storyteller), 57, 58
Porphyry (philosopher), 10
Possidius (biographer), 6
Power, Kim, *Veiled Desire: Augustine on Women*, 89
predestination, 5
pride, examination of, 70
Prodigal Son metaphor, 55–56
punishment, views of, 20–21

R

rationality, 34–35, 67
rebellion against God, 27
rest, 78
Retractiones (St. Augustine), 6, 8
rhetorical style, 17
Rome, 4, 43
Rousseau, Jean-Jacques, *Confessions*, 81

S

Saint Augustine: Stanford Encyclopedia of
    Philosophy Web site, 89
self, knowing, 66
senses and temptation, 69
sexual sin, attitude toward, 25–26, 29, 82–84
Sheed, F. J. (translator), 89
Simplicianus (teacher), 55
sin. *See* original sin; sexual sin, attitude toward
soothsayers, views on, 34
soul, 19
St. Augustine's Confessions (Robert O'Connell), 89
style and language
    autobiography, 59, 81–82
    dialogue form, 76

    praise to God, 16
    rhetorical style, 17
    tone of self-mockery, 49
synopsis, 13–14

T

"Take and read.", 86
temptations, worldly, 49–50, 68, 69
theater, weakness for, 23, 30, 70
themes. *See also* language
    death and change, 60–61
    dreams, 32
    follies of humans, 20
    habit, giving up bad, 46–47, 58, 63
    original sin, 5, 18–19, 29–30, 83–84
    Platonic ascent of soul, 53, 69, 78–79
    sexual lust, 29–30
    "signs," 19
    sin, 25–26, 27, 29, 32, 82–84
time, nature of, 71–73
translations, 89
truth
    autobiography and, 81–82
    expression of, 42
    love and, 66

V

Vandals, 5–6
vanity, 40, 75–76
Veiled Desire: Augustine on Women (Kim Power), 89
Verecundus (friend), 57–58, 60–61
Victorinus (rhetor), 55, 58
Visigoths, 4
visions
    beatific, 53, 54, 69, 73, 75
    at Ostia, 64

W

water imagery, 43–44
Web sites
    CliffsNotes, 88, 89
    St. Augustine-related, 89
will, human, views of, 35, 52–53
women, attitudes toward, 36, 83–84
wrongdoing, love of, 27–28

Y

*Young Augustine, The: An Introduction to the Confessions
    of St. Augustine* (John O'Meara), 89